BIRTH OF A NATION

J. L. Rose

iUniverse, Inc.
Bloomington

Birth of a Nation

iUniverse books may be ordered through booksellers or by contacting:

iUniverse
1663 Liberty Drive
Bloomington, IN 47403
www.iuniverse.com
1-800-Authors (1-800-288-4677)

ISBN: 978-1-4620-1109-4 (pbk)
ISBN: 978-1-4620-1111-7 (ebk)

Printed in the United States of America

iUniverse rev. date: 4/27/2011

About the Author

Julio Rose was born Panama City, Republic of Panama, November 1954, where he studied theology at the Franciscan Theological seminary at Boquete, in the Chiriquí province.

He migrated to the United States in April of 1974, took up residence in Los Angeles, California, then to Brooklyn, New York, Augusta, Georgia, Columbia, South Carolina.

He moved to Columbia, South Carolina, thereafter where he attended Benedict College, earning a Bachelor of Arts degree in Political Science and Public Administration. He then picked up residence in Central America.

His expertise is in linguistics and is fluent in the English, Spanish and Arabic languages. Areas o travel includes Central America, Asia, Europe, Australia and Puerto Rico.

Contents

Introduction

Religion has become one of the most powerful things in the life of most people. Religion was first brought by westerners, who set out to conquer lands as they left the caves of Europe and Asia. The most celebrated of such in the Americas, is Christopher Columbus, who upon his arrival, he called it "New world.

The so-called New world would then need a governing, digestible to the Caucasian palate. They quickly found a solution, and opted on a New world order. The rules to be established, would have to be embedded in the subconscious of the victims by the victor, this will be called the New Testament.

It must be clear to the reader that, when Columbus arrived in the Americas, he was unlettered, unable to read and write. Columbus arrived in Spain only seven years before he arrived in the Americas, 1485. Spain had just got out of a war with the Moors, and was still suffering the effects of such war.

Another thing that must be clear, is that after spending so many years in the caves of Asia and the wintery deserts of Europe; it is perfectly understandable why Caucasians would refer to everything as "New". Then again, there is nothing new under the sun, **Ecclesiastes 1: 9.**

Religion is the single most diabolical and dangerous idiosyncrasy one could ever experience. Many will say that religion is sometimes good because of its intention, I maintain that, the road to death and destruction is paved with good intention.

Over the years, we have witnessed how the Caucasian (cavemen) has taken much delight in the art of deception, an art not limited toward others, but the self as well. This deception is seen in every aspect of western culture, military geniuses at west point, firmly believe the Trojan horse trick to be military genius. Cavemen believe that deception is the "art of war", and as the trickster said, "power perceived is power achieved".

These tricksters have not considered that every action (cause, percussion) has a reaction (effect, repercussion). The western culture is reaping what they have sowed over the years. They have the knowledge of the science of opposites (good and evil), yet they did not observe the proper balance of the same. Instead they wanted to satisfy their wicked desires.

The time to pay the piper is rapidly approaching, can the westerners live up to payment? Their society is about to become the "Police State" they hate so much, and of which they so much accused China and Russia. They moved too far right on the symmetry scale, without considering that anything in excess produces an effect opposite to that intended.

copyright Julio L. Rose

Then there arose a synagogue (lodge) called temple (shrine) of the Liberty-ines (Freemasons). The waters you saw where the harlot (Liberty statue) sits are people, multitudes (of Africans, Latinos, Caucasians, Orientals, Arabs, etc) and languages, **Acts 6: 9; Rev 17: 15.**

A child is born

You shall conceive and bear son, no razor shall come upon his head (a hairy rebel), **Judges 13: 5**.

The King (dragon) stood before the woman who was ready to give birth, to devour (exile, destroy) the child as soon as it was born, **Revelation 12:4**.

The woman fled into the wilderness (cave), **Revelation 12: 6**.

It came to pass, at the time for giving birth, twins (Romulus and Remus; Cain and Abel) were in her womb. When she was giving birth one put out his hand, this one came out first, **Genesis 38: 28**.

The first one came out <u>red all over,</u> like a hairy garment, **Genesis 25:25.**

She bore a male child who was to rule all nations with a rod of iron. The child then declares: I come as a thief in the night, **Rev 16: 15**.

The smell of my son is like the smell of the animal of the filth (field), **Genesis 27:27**.

The King said to his servants; bind (**Oedi**) him hand and foot and cast him into utter darkness, **Matthew 22: 13.**

Every religious (cultural) philosophy invariably starts with the birth of a child. The story of Muhammad starts with this little Arab child who was taken into the wilderness of the desert, and raised there. The story of Jesus has a very similar tone; he was taken into the cave (mange) and raised there. The story of Moses has a very similar tune; and the stories of Zeus and Krishna also bear a striking resemblance.

As we regress in the annals of history, we see that the story of Oedipus is of the same tune; he was sent to the caves and saved there by a passer-by who would later be dubbed a Good Samaritan. The story of Zeus is very similar, like Jesus he was taken by his mother to the island of Crete, where he was raised in secrecy.

It must be made clear to the reader that, all of the stories you have just red, represent the same group of people. Muhammad, Jesus, Moses, Oedipus, Zeus and all the characters in question, symbolize a different episode of the life of those we have come to know as cavemen.

The people of the cave are known today in the scientific arena as Homo sapiens. These cavemen are direct descendants of another group called Homo erectus, the African albinos that gave birth to the Caucasian race. The latter are albinos who were exiled from Egypt, centuries before any form of religion was ever known. The most celebrated story of the albino's departure from Egypt is known as the Exodus.

Homo Sapiens: Caucasian
Homo Erectus: Albino (hybrid)
Exodus: Caucasian journey to cave
Hijra: Arab journey to cave and desert

The story of Adam and Eve is only one of so many versions of the same saga, the outcast of the genetic defective albinos from the Egyptian (Garden of Eden) territory. The many versions of the same story give us the word versatile (many versions). The Caucasian race has glamorized its migration from Egypt, in such fashion that it couldn't but evoke and inspire emotion.

The story of Moses would make it appear as if the albinos escaped Egypt against the king's (Pharaoh's) will, these albinos were expelled from Egypt. And this story is also dramatized as Adam (Edom) and Eve cast out of Carth-age (Garden) of Eden.

The ritualistic drama known as bull-fighting is a dramatization of this expulsion. The bull is known as two-horned one, the two horns symbolize the knowledge of two, good and evil. This knowledge is also known as science of opposites. Egypt was famously known as Khart-Akh (Carthage), from whence came the words Khart-n (cartoon and garden).

Khart-akh: Carthage (Egypt)
Khart-n: Garden (of Eden)
Khart-n: Cartoon (hieroglyph)

Cartoon is the name of the language Caucasians call hieroglyph, which is later animated for children. The garden (of Eden) is a title attributed to Thebes (Egypt) by religious groups; another title is E-Thebe-a (Utopia or Ethiopia). The soldiers, who watched its borders in order to keep out the cavemen, were called Khart (guard). These guards are symbolized by the black bull used in the bull-fighting ritual.

Khart-n: Cartoon, Garden (of Eden)
Khart: Guard Soldiers posted at border preventing cavemen's re entry into Khart-Akh (Carthage: Egypt)

By some accounts, these soldiers numbered about two-hundred forty-thousand (240,000). Then why does the

Caucasian religious organizer claim that Moses ran and the Pharaoh opposed it? The truth is they were cast out because of their many genetic flaws and unruly behavior. The writer finds the need to narrate the story without all the exaggerated emotion usually found in religion. Remember, religion is the glamorization (deification) of a race and/or culture.

Every single piece of literature demonstrates that the cavemen were expelled, they did not escape. It appears as an escape when the story is been trivialized, a typical Caucasian pastime. Remember the cavemen were once called children by Egyptians, and that is the reason fairy-tale stories are all about children.

The story of the cavemen starts with the announcement to the king and his wife, who are blood relatives (cousins). She is pregnant and will soon deliver a child. The child is of course illegitimate, since the parents are relatives, therefore must be aborted (put to death). The announcement is given to the king and his wife.

The hymnal narrating the story of Oedipus teaches that King Lai, Oedipus' father is cousin to his wife Jocasta. There is a forbidden union, the union of close relatives. Their children would be genetically defective and/or deficient, making him albino (Homo erectus). This is the reason for which the king had to exile the child.

The rod of iron with which all nations shall be ruled, is the and world power military arsenal, an idea brought to us by the European desire to rule the world. This is also seen in the oath of initiation taken by the Jesuit order. The story of the king and his wife, who is about to give birth to a child, continues, to the point of complete and utter enmity. This rivalry is culturally and typically known as "the battles of the sexes".

> The King (dragon) was enraged with the woman; he (king) persecuted the woman who gave birth to a male child. **Rev 12: 17**.

> I (Christian culture) will put enmity (battle of sexes) between you (male) and the woman (female), between your seed (gender) and her seed (gender). He will bruise your head, and you will bruise his heel, **Gen 3: 15**.

The fleeing of the woman into the caves (wilderness) is known but not understood by Christian culture, as Mary flees into the cave (manger) and gives birth to Jesus. This fleeing is exactly what will happen with the arrival of father-alism (federalism), better known as white male supremacy.

After the child's birth, the king finds himself in a dilemma, he later decides on sending the child into the caves of Eurasia. The above biblical quotes show the reason for which the king attempts to kill or exile the first male child. The king calls unto his servants and issues a decree.

The mere appearance of the cavemen causes the skin to shudder as people looked at them. This is nothing new for many a tales have been made up from their appearance. The story of the Leper-khauns (leprechauns) is a classical example. The genetic make-up of the cavemen is the reason they are cold (arctic) blooded creatures.

> The child was born at the break of day, and ere the nightfall had stolen Apollo's herd, **Birth of Hermes.**

The darkness into which the child or cavemen is thrown, is called sleep synonymous to death. This is the central theme in the darkness (sleep) of the cavemen, is shown to us in the hymnal suffered by Abraham. The word swoon is the plural form of the word "swine", the symbol or icon of the Hebrew race. It was later changed to Lycaon (Lycian), but pronounced Legion.

> When the sun (wisdom) was going down

(diminishing light, wisdom), a deep sleep (ignorance) fell upon Abram (child); behold, horror and great (age of) darkness (cave life) fell upon him, **Gen 15: 12.**

When the darkness overshadowed him, he saw a star (light in the darkness); and said, is this my lord (culture, altar)? When it set he said, I don' t appreciate that which sets (vanishes). Then he saw the rising moon and said, is this my lord (altar, values, culture)? When it set he said, if my lord does not guide (initiate) me, I will be among the ignorant (lost). When he saw the sun (light, wisdom) he said, is this my lord? Is this not the greatest? **Quran 6:** 77 – 79.

Abraham the metaphor is a narrative explaining the Egyptian enlightenment of the cavemen, the cult of the sun (god). It must be clear to the reader that the afrikans (Egyptians) never believed the sun to be this supernatural spook, known to many as god. The sun is only a symbol or icon of that which gives life and takes life, the alpha and the omega.

They (cavemen) were forced in the clefts of the valleys, in caves of the earth and rocks. Among the bushes they brayed, under the nettles they nestled. They were sons of fools, yes, sons of vile (violent) men; they were scourged from the land**.** A base and nameless brood (offspring); they were driven out of the land, **Job 30: 6-8.**

When a thousand years have passed, Sat-n (Seth's children) will be released from his cave (prison), **Rev 20:**7.

A Nikh-il (Nigel, Angel: treacherous prince)

descended from heaven (elite) and rolled back the stone from the cave (door), **Matthew 28: 2.**

The words valleys, violent and vile are variants of the word Val. Valhalla is the dwelling place of the Vallen (fallen) warriors, according to Nors myth. Val: Valley, Val-Hall (Valhalla), vile (violent), villain. The voice in the wilderness is a literary form of expression; it explains the caveman's saga, a cry (bray) in the wild, a bray (voice) in the wilderness.

The return from the cave is highlighted in the story of Oedipus who murders his father the king, only to take his own mother as his wife. The child returns to his household, not having the slightest idea that he is the son of the king he murdered some time before. He questions the servant that brought him to the household when he was a child. The servant is represented by the oracle Oedipus seized because the same refused to reveal the truth about Oedipus' fate (saga).

The famous vow of silence is the great secrecy held in masonry; no one is supposed to reveal the true story of the nature of the cavemen. This oath of secrecy is taken during their pledge of initiation to the fraternity or brotherhood.

The story becomes even more bizarre when Oedipus (cavemen) marries his mother, thus creating genetically defective off-spring. We must remember that Oedipus children are the product of two people who are closely related. Then, he mates with his mother, hence the phrase mother fucker.

Mother fucker: The Oedipus complex

The priest will look at the plague (albinism), and if it is deeper than the skin (transparent), and has yellow (blond) thin hair, then the priest shall declare him unclean, **Leviticus 13: 30.**

The albinos were to be known later as Homo erectus,

parents of Homo sapiens, known today as (Caucasian). There are many superstitious beliefs concerning the albino, also there are many scientific evidence that justified casting them out of Africa. The expulsion of the Hebrews from Egypt**,** known to many as the Exodus, is a glamorized version of this exile of genetically deficient people.

The people of the earth are said to have evolved from all the Eli-ments (elements) of the earth, possessing all of these Eli-ments (elements) in their constitution (gold, silver, iron, zinc, etc.); all except the albinos (Homo erectus) and their children the Caucasian (Homo sapiens).

> On this account of the creation, the gods seemed bent on experimenting with the various metals, and oddly enough proceeding downward from the from the excellent, to the good, to the worse and so on…When they had tried gold, they went to silver. This second race of silver was very inferior to the first. They had little intelligence that they could not keep from injuring each other (**Edith Hamilton**, **1940**).

The gods in reference by Ms Hamilton are none other than the people of yore who are venerated by contemporary culture as Khu-Fu (Cheops, Chiapas, Capo), known also as the father of medicine. The father of medicine is famously known in the hymnal as Melchizedek and Jacob; Roman culture knows him as Esculapius, while Greek culture knows him as Hippocrates.

The albinos and their descendants the Caucasians were referred to as children by the Egyptians. The word child is derived from the word Celt (Celtic). The place called Child-ia (Chaldea) is named after these children. There is a science named after this Celt (child). This science is called Celt-ion, is written and pronounced Chelation. The same consists of the study and measure of metals in the blood stream. **Celt-ion**

(Chelation) is the study of metals/minerals (mercury, lead, iron, etc) in the Celt's (Caucasian) blood stream.

The above quote from Edith Hamilton appears to be a scientific metaphor of the origin of the Caucasian race, and the reason they are such cold-blooded creatures. Again, his wickedness can be attributed to his genetic constitution. The metals, to which Ms Hamilton alludes, represent the different ethnic groups that emanated from the very dark colored race of people. Obviously, people are not made of gold and silver, their blood may contain some of these minerals.

The word metal is derived from the Egyptian word Mit, a variant of the name of the cow-goddess Mut, one of the many symbolic mothers of the Caucasian race, and from whence they derive the word mut-r (mother). The land into which the albinos were exiled was named Mut-terrain, hence the descriptive Mediterranean race. Mut: Symbolic Mut-r (mother) of the cavemen; Mut: Met-al, Met-terrain (Mediterranean).

The genetic non-pigmented system or imbalance of the Caucasian is the purpose of chelation. The word Celt later yielded the word kill. This word evolved from the Greek word Cleo/Cloe (Chloe), which later gave us the Latin word caelu-m meaning heaven.

Heaven consists of these people of the cave, a fact easily confirmed, **Matthew 19:14,** Celo (Chile): Haven (Havana); Celt-n (Child-n): Chaldean. The word have-n means opulence or wealth, the haves and the haves not, the alpha and the omega.

The Latin word caelu-m (heaven), Caucasian heaven, is from whence we learn the words caelum-ny (calumny) and caelu-mity (calamity), the arrival of the cavemen. This caelumity (calamity) is also known as the opening of Pandora's jar, Caelu-m: Heaven; Caelu-m-t (calamity): Haven-ly; Caelu-m-n (calumny): Haven-ly myth.

The people are one (nation), and they all speak one idiom. Let us (cavemen) go down and there <u>con-fuse</u> (melting-pot) their idiom, that they may not comprehend each other, **Genesis 11: 4, 7.**

This photo is one of the many Olmec Heads found throughout areas of Mexico. This should lay to rest the myth that the African race came here by slavery.

There are many of these heads found in Mexican territory. The Mexicans would not build a monument to foreigners without first building one representing them. The dark skin race of people is ubiquitous, and were not all brought to the west via slavery. The ubiquitous idiom called hieroglyph is the same one used by the Aztecs and Maya people, **Genesis 11:7**.

You will conceive and gave birth to a son; no razor will be used upon his head, **Judges 13: 5**. The first one came out red all over, like a hairy garment, **Genesis 25: 25**. The smell of my son is (as) the smell of the animals of the field, **Genesis 27: 27.** The king (Lai) said to his servants, bind him hand and foot (bigfoot), take him away and cast him into utter darkness (cave), **Matt 22:13**.

They lived in the clefts of the valleys, in caves of the earth and rocks. Among the bushes they brayed, under the nettles they nestled. They were sons of fools, yes, sons of vile (violent) men; they were scourged from the land, **Job 30: 6.**

They have become filled with every kind of wickedness, evil, greed and depravity. They are full of envy, murder, strife, deceit and malice… Insolent, arrogant and boastful… They disobey their parents (ancestors); they are senseless, faithless, heartless, ruthless, **Romans 1: 29 – 31**.

The above Biblical quotes explain the birth of and propensity for violence of those of Caucasian genum. This violence is manifested today as domestic violence, among other things; where the woman becomes the enemy of the kingdom or culture. This is further corroborated in the personification of Caucasian culture, Jesus himself. The hymnal (Bible) is very clear on this point.

I (Christianity, cave culture) come to turn man against father, daughter against her mother, a daughter-in-law against her mother-in-law; a man's i will be the members of his own household (family feud), **Matthew 10: 34**.

The father who is in heaven represents the elite people, as the word have-n suggests, opulence or possessing wealth. To live lavishly, is to live in have-n (heaven). The father is the king and his son the prince, as suggested by the word "father-lis (federal)".

The father (Zeus) is in have-n (opulence).

Have: To possess, opulence
Have-n: People or children of the opulent

The father and son are also known as "Dad and Dude", both words are evolved from the name Daud (David), the king and alleged father of Solomon. This is clearly the reason Jesus the dude is called "son of Daud (David).

The opulence mentioned above, is what we have come to know as the "American dream", is the reason the capitalists usually brag of their possessions. Again, the manger in which this child was born and reared is nothing but the cold and humid caves; this cave causes a dermal abnormality called mange.

Mange is a dermal abnormality, a word that evolved from the word "manu (cave creature), from the Egyptian language. The hairy caveman Rome-d (roamed) the Egyptian border, creating a new mixed-race called Mur (Moor) today. Many of these settled in what is known today as Morocco and Mauritania, named after them. Another group that settled in this area are called "Berbers (Barbarians)".

It is imperative that the origin of the word Moor be established. This name evolved from the name Mur, one of the four sons of goddess Nikh, the cave goddess, something will be seen later as we read this material. The word and concept of

Mur (Moor) was later identified with being tied to the cave, a fact one can see in the word "mooring line", a line used to tie or attach something. From this concept we also evolved the word "moron", meaning a fool and "maraud", meaning seize, capture, steal, rob, etc.

> Mur (Moor): Morocco, Mauritania, maurad,
> mooring (tide to cave) moron

The word clean like the word clone, were derived from the Latin word caelu (cielo) meaning haven (heaven). To be a clone is to be made in the "image and likeness" of the god in heaven. The Caucasian was grafted in the image and likeness of Africans of antiquity. It must be borne in mind that have-n (opulence) is an exclusive club created by Caucasians for their pleasure. Haven (heaven) has nothing to do with Mother Nature.

> Clean-ic: Clone, clinic
> Haven-ly: Opulently, prodigiously, wealthy

The cavemen at birth, is as hairy as a bear. The Berber's entire body was shaved, and they sometimes bled because of dermal abnormalities such as acne, psoriasis, seborrhea, etc. Their bleeding skin was wipe with a white rag and hung outside, which explains the peppermint gyrating outside the "Berber shave (Barber shop)".

Traditionally, when a person becomes adherent or devotee of a temple or philosophy, he shaves his head. This tradition is taken from the Egyptian initiation of the cavemen. Caucasian philosophy writers are now re-inventing the meaning of this ritual. The above quote is the reason Caucasians had to be cleansed by the Egyptians; it is the reason the renegade child had no razor come upon his head.

The cleansing of these cavemen is an attempt by the

Egyptians, to incorporate them to the rest of the world's societies. This cleansing process is referred as healed (w-hole), pronounced holy. The apron worn by the hairy (Berber) man, is known in Masonic circles as the sheepskin, and represents the fig leaves used by Adam (Edom) to cover his nikht-ness (nakedness, ignorance).

> He was a hairy man, girt with a leather girdle (apron), **2 Kings 1:8**.

The mere appearance of the cavemen causes the skin to shudder as people looked at them. This is nothing new, for many a tales have been made up highlighting this appearance. Oedipus was told by the oracle that endogamy (incest) with his mother, would produce children that would horrify their on-looker. The story of the Leper-khauns (leprechauns) is a classical example. The genetic make-up of the cavemen is the reason they are cold (arctic) blooded creatures.

The sheep-skin represents the status of the cavemen, meaning, that his lamb-like condition must be that of submission to his God (grafter, progenitor). His failure to submit is one of the reasons he is cast out of Egypt. The condition of the planet under his leadership justifies his expulsion away from superior thinkers. As the saying goes, Mary (mother of Jesus) had a little lamb whose flesh (fleece, sheepskin) was white as snow (a leper).

The sheep-skin is the symbol of the alpha Jesus (cavemen), while the wolf is his alter-ego or omega. The phrase wolf in sheep's clothing is in reference to the Caucasian race, he is the alpha (wolf) and who wears the sheepskin (Masonic apron).

The word sheep (shave, shop) is taken from the Egyptian word sif (suf, soph, sapiens), meaning wisdom (light), while the word wolf, is the Scandinavian pronunciation of the word Alpha, pronouncing it Ulaf (olive). Alpha (Ulaf): Wolf; Suf (soph): Sapiens, Sheep (Sheba); Alpha in Omega: Wolf in sheep's clothing.

> The light (alpha) shines in the darkness (omega) and the darkness comprehends it not, **John 1: 5.**

The alpha (alpha: alpine, albino) race were produced in Egypt and exiled into the caves. This return is marked by Oedipus' encounter with and assassination of his father, hence the family feud. The light shining in the darkness, is symbolized by the star (light) that shines in the dark, the star allegedly followed by Shadrak, Meschak and Abednego or three Magi.

> Out of Egypt I called my son (Manu or cavemen), **Mathew 2: 15 and Hosea 1:11.**

> Egypt (Thebes is) also where our Lord (Jesus) was crucified (cast into the darkness of the cave or wilderness)**, Rev 11: 8.**

The compound word Oed-pus (Oedipus) means, moored by the ankle (bound-by-the-foot), **Matthew 22:13**; this phrase was to change later to mean bondage (prison). Besides this, the scientific community would also change the meaning of the word Yti (Yeti, Oed) from tied to swollen. The binding of the child by the ankle, did not allow for proper blood circulation, reason for which the ankle became swollen, hence the phrase "Big-foot".

> Iti (Yeti): Bind (bondage), to tie
> Itis: Swollen, inflammation
> Oed-pus: Swollen foot (Big-foot)

The maddening rage mentioned will become manifested

soon as the cavemen are released from their dwelling, the cave. The life of the cave is enough to drive any sane person into the anger (cold-blooded) suffered by the cavemen. The propensity for violence, combined with this maddening rage, makes the cavemen a very dangerous creature.

The heaven or city is called also by the name Hill. The hall on the hill where all the val-n (fallen) warriors dwell is called Val-Hall (Valhalla), the Common (non-elite) live at the foot of the hill which is called Hell. The elite class (gods) lives on the Zion (Zenith) of the mountain.

Hill: Top of mountain (heaven)
Hall: Dwelling place of the Elite
Hell: Dwelling place of the Common

The story of this exile (Exodus) is the opening chapter of Hebrew culture, who they prefer to call themselves Czeu-s (Jews). The word Jew is a phonetic variant of the word Czeu, fore-runner of the name Zeus. The under-world or darkness into which the child was cast is described in the above narrative; this darkness is the cave.

The story of Oedipus and his father King Lai, is the most visible and clear example of the ape-man-able (abominable snowman). This man is also seen once a year under the name Sat-Nikh-La (Seth the treacherous prince), known to most as Santa Claus. The king opted to exile the child because he is illegitimate (bastard: leper); he is an albino who was brought about by incest (endogamy). The word bastard is of Egyptian origin, and the same means white (albino) god.

> Let us make our father (in heaven) drink wine, and we lie (endogamy, incest) with him, that we may preserve the seed (gene) of our father (who is in haven), **Gen 19: 32.**

God (father) made manu in his image (physical appearance, resemblance) and likeness (nature), **Gen 1:26**.

I (cavemen, albino) was brought forth in iniquity (endogamy, incest, monarchy), and in sin (ignorance) my mother conceived (grafted) me, **Psalms 51: 5.**

The in-equity (iniquity) mentioned above is known today as endogamy in the field of science, while in the religious circle it is called incest. Endogamy is the act of mating with close family relatives, thus causing a genetic retraction, we call it in-equity (imbalance) or in religious circles iniquity.

The afore-mentioned concept is widely practiced among Caucasian, particularly among politicians and is called monarchy; the only way for the Caucasian gene could ever exist. This topic is one very few people, if any, would want to discuss. The above mentioned Biblical quote is proof of this orgy that brought the Caucasian into existence.

Incest: Religious jargon
Monarchy: Political jargon
Endogamy: Scientific jargon

The creation of the Caucasian race or cavemen is known also under the name alchemy. This word is the superlative form of the word Leuchemia (leukemia), meaning whiteness, brightness or fairness. The word leuchemia (alchemy) is also the word that provides us with the word Leuci-fer (Lucifer), meaning brightly fair-race.

Alchemy: Luchemia (white blood)
Leuchi-fer: Lucifer (as white as snow)
Leuchi-mia: Brightness, whiteness, fairness

The story of Tarzan the Abo-min (Trojan the Ape-man) is presented wrapped in such beautiful package that it is difficult to resist. This is only another extrapolation of the cavemen's saga. Notice how the Caucasian used adulteration and alteration of words, to change the perception of the aforementioned stories,

Trojan: Tarzan
Abomin: Apeman

Amazingly, the word Trojan is a phonetic variant of the word Tarzan, the ape-man or ape-man-able (abomin-able) snowman. Tarzan, as the story says was an Anglo-ish (English) raised by apes. Can you now see the parallel between Caucasian scientific findings and literature?

The above mentioned words, are derived from the Egyptian word Tarkh, meaning, left in oblivion (cave). This word is from where we obtain the name we know today as Turkh (Turkey). This word also gave us the words trick, trek (journey to cave), dark, etc. Turkey is the gateway between Asia (mother) and Europe (daughter).

Turkh (Turkey): Trick, torch, trek, dark, etc

The word tarkh (dark) also yields the word dark-n (dragon), the title of the serpent representing the Caucasian (cavemen). The serpent is the spitting cobra, which spits acid directly to the eyes of its victim, rendering him/her blind. That is the meaning of the fire (acid), the poison spewed by Caucasian culture rendering its members blind or state of ignorance.

Dark-n (Dragon): African spitting cobra

Caucasians are experts in the art of deception, changing perception through deception. Such was the case of Odysseus, known among the gods as the cunning trickster. The perception of the people has been changed, evident in the change of language.

> Let us (cavemen) go down (from the city on a hill) and there confuse their (other cultures) language. **Gen 11: 7.**

> You (cavemen) have perverted the words, **Jeremiah 23: 36.**

The word leuce is the product of an Egyptian word, Lukh (Luxor), and the same is integrated into the Spanish language as leche, meaning, milk. It is derived from the name of the Scandinavian god Luke (Loki: snowy white), the cunning trickster and trouble-maker among the gods. The word milk is also of Egyptian origin, originally written m-lukh, it means possessor of fair or faro (brightness, light). The Arabic language pronounces this word Maalik meaning, possessor, owner (of light, knowledge).

Lukh (Luke): Loki, Leuch, Leche (Milk)
M-luk (Malik): Possessor of light (wisdom)

We later lived and learn that the language and culture of the people the world over became somewhat extinct. The word Olympus, heaven of god Czeu (Zeus, Jew) and his Olympians, finds its name in the word lymph, the lymphatic fluid that contains bacteria. Are these mere coincidences? Certainly not, the genetic deficiency of Homo erectus and Homo sapiens is widely told in literature.

Lymph (U-lymph): Olympus

Other versions of the same story, different names,

have it that Hercules removed the stone, the insider then was Prometheus. No matter the name of the protagonists (antagonists: knowledge robber); the story still carries the same central theme, the stealing of fire (wisdom) and giving the same to Manu (children of the cave or of Israel).

It is said in the hymnal that, God created Manu (cavemen) in his image and likeness. This image and likeness is the albino race, an exact replica of the original "human", remember, God is a man, (**Exodus 15:3**) and so is his duplicate (**Genesis 1:26**). The replica in question is known also as Double or Diablo, the Latin word for devil. The word devil went on to become the word devil-itate (debilitate), meaning lacking the nectar of life, a nectar the Greek language refers to as melanin.

Double/Diablo: Image and likeness
Devil (debilitate): Lacking nectar or melanin

The above words are all derived from the Latin word devs (dos), meaning two (2), the alpha and the omega. This is derived from the Egyptian word Tua, Greek Theo, the name of the science of opposites, known as good and evil. The word devs gives us the words David, Devil and Devine.

Tau: Theo
Tau: Deu (Dev)
Dev (David): Dev-ine and Dev-il
Tva (dves): Theo (Two opposites)
Idev-s (idea): God (inspiration)
Idev-m (idiom): Expressed psyche

Unlike the word idiom, the word language is derived from the Latin word lengua, meaning tongue. This is related to phonetics, or sounds produced by the vocal chords, and nothing else. Then we have that the word idio-t is an antonym of the word idio-m.

It must be clear that this grammar is originally and uniquely Egyptian, and is not of Greek origin as many Caucasians allege. They must also remember that, the Hell-enist (Hellenist) or Greek society was originated by an Egyptian man name San-Rus-Ra in the year 1927 BAD (Before Anno Domino). Strangely, the word Hel-n (Hellen) means, children or people of Hel (hell).

Hel (Hal: hell): Goddess of death, Nors myth

It is essential that we explain the word ideu-m (idiom). This word is a variant of the again Latin word ideu-s (idea), meaning gods. The Romans learned this word from their Egyptian counterpart. The Egyptian word for this is Tua; the Greeks pronounce it Theo and English Two. This word is the name of the science of good and evil, the concept of opposites.

Anno domino is the year when Caucasian power is officially set on the historical scene. Any event prior to this year is known as pre-history, while any event following this year is known as history. The Caucasian is so deep into his own lies, that at this point he believes the same.

History: Events following year one C. E.
Pre-history**:** Events prior to the year one C. E.

Based on the above, one can safely conclude that the lack of nectar (melanin) is a debilitating process rendering its victim a walking dead, hence the phrase "firstborn from the dead". This explains why the Greek literary language refers to these people, as mortals, why Jesus alleges to have been born from the dead (mortal or albino).

Let the dead (albinos, mortals) bury their dead, **Matthew 8: 22.**

The dead referred to in the above quote, is the albino. The Egyptian word for these albinos is Bas, meaning dead or albino, hence the phrases bas-away, pronounced pass-away, and bas-o-fir, pronounced Passover. This word explains the origin of the words pus and pus-itive, a word disguised as good. It is the feast-of-Val (festival), the spring celebration, meaning death to life. This is in reference to the death of the winter and the life or birth of the spring.

Bas (pus): Dead, leper
Bas-away: Dead, deceased
Bas-o-fir: Passover (Winter-o-spring)

The lack of nectar (melanin) suffered by the Caucasian race is better known as leprosy, this has become unacceptable to the Caucasian race, who opted to disguise the same with a litany of pseudonyms. The white or paleness means recessive, regressive, inactivity, inaction or death; this went on to become the symbol for inactivity or surrender during battle, the white flag.

W-hite: Absence of color, energy or life

The word white is an adulteration of the name of the Biblical Heth (Hades), father of Hedonism and of the Hittites. This word is prefixed with the letter "w" in an attempt to disguise the facts, and so is the word Hur (whore), father of the Horites (Horae). All of the afore-mentioned are of Caucasoid origin.

Hit (Heth, Hate): Hades (w-hite)
Hur (Horae): Horites (w-Hore)

The word nectar (melanin) is the Caucasian pronunciation of the Egyptian word Nikht-r, meaning darkness and used symbolically to say ignorance. This word is derived from the name of goddess Nikh-t, the cave (darkness and ignorance). Strangely, a variant of this word is the word Nakh (ankh), meaning life, the complete opposite, hence the word Nakh-tive (negative).

Nakh: Life, wisdom
Nikh: Death, ignorance

The two main words mentioned above gave origin to the words negative (life) and positive (death), meaning life and death respectively. They are the principal reason the electrical system has black and white wires. The basic electrical wiring system consists of two main wires, both of which are known as nakht-f (negative), the live wire and bast-f (positive) or dead wire.

Caucasian culture has changed the meaning of both of these words. Firstly, the word nakh-tive (negative) is from the Egyptian word nakh (ankh) meaning life. The word bas-tive (positive) is also of Egyptian origin and the same means albinism or death. The word nakht is the antonym of the word Nikht (Nick) the goddess of cave (darkness) and symbolic mother of the cavemen. Her name is also associated with the word night, the darkness of the cave, hence the words necro and negro, often applied to the darker skin people and to the dead.

Live/life: Nakht-f (negative), black wire
Death/pass: Bast (positive), white wire, (albino)

The word bast is the Egyptian word for albinism and/or those who are lepers, the dead from which Jesus claims birth in **Revelation 1: 5.**

The word leper is originated in the earlier version of Jesus, under his name of antiquity, the god of wine and vegetation,

Bacchus, who the Romans call Liber. This word is a variant of the word Alb/Lab, the same word from whence we derive alb-n (Laban, albino), hence the name Labanon (Lebanon). The Czeus (Jewish) community pronounces the words Lab (Levi) and Laban (Levin).

Lab, Laban: Levi, Levin, Lebanon
Laban had seven (7) children, **Gen 40:25**

The seven (7) children mentioned above, are only a metaphor of the seven main albino gods representing cavemen culture. These seven gods are known as seven (7) Kings in the book of Revelation, and have each a day of the week to honor each of them.

There are seven (7) altars (cultures, world powers), and also seven kings, **Rev 15: 1.**

Jack fell down and lost his crown.

Hold on (Jack) to what you have, so that no one will take your crown…the new Jerusalem (new world order), **Revelation 3: 11, 12**.

What is clear is that Caucasians attempt to confuse the multitude of people alleging that Christians and Jews have separate religious agendas. The truth is that the only agenda ever-present is Caucasian male supremacy and control of the world's resources. Was not Jesus a Czeu (Jew)? He was a Czeu (Jew), not a Christian, **John 4:** 7.

The seven altars, not churches as alleged by Caucasians, are their cultural symbols and values. In the Bible these are called Ephesus, Smyrna, Pergamus, Thyatira, Sardis, Philadelphia and Laodicea.

The word altar is derived from the Latin word Alt,

meaning highest (tallest) values. The Latin language borrowed it from the Arabic Ali, meaning high, while the Roman culture called it Ult-r (alter, ultra), meaning high. **Altar** (Alter, Ultra): Monument to society's highest cultural value.

The seven altars (cultures, gods) are:

1. Ephesus: Sun, Atum, the Sun god
1. Smyrna: Luna, the Moon goddess
2. Pergamus: Odin, Mercury, Hermes
3. Thyatira: Tiu, Mars, the War god
4. Sardis Thor, Jupiter, Zeus
5. Philadelphia Frya, Venus, the love goddess
6. Laodicea: Saturn, Sab, Chronis, Dragon

The seven gods mentioned above represent the seven days (ages) in which the world (Caucasian empire) was created. They are the participants of the drama we know as "Seven against Thebes". In this drama they are known under alternate names, remember that names may change from story to story, the central theme doesn't.

Seven against Thebes, the names are:

1. Polynieces
1. Capaneus
2. Eteocles
3. Hippomeddon
4. Parthanopaeus
5. Tydeus
6. Adrastus

The seven aforementioned gods are also known in children fairy tales as Snow-White and the seven alphas (elves, albinos), later known as dwarfs. Snow-white is the harlot that sits upon the waters, memorialized as statue of Liberty, **Rev 17:1**.

The one predominant god in contemporary culture is god

Dionysus (Jesus), also known as Bacchus. Roman or Latin culture calls him Liber, he is usually found accompanied by an entourage of twelve female called Bacchantes, Horae (whore), Maenads, Bacchantes or Libertines.

The culture of the Bacchantes is called Bacchanal, while the culture of the Libertines is called Liberalism. When Bacchus is called Liber, his women are called Libertines, **Acts 6: 9;** when he is called Bacchus, they are called Bacchantes. They are called Maenads when he is referred to as Dionysus.

> Dionysus: Maenads
> Bacchus: Bacchantes, Bacchanal
> Liber (Leper): Libertines, liberalism

The afore-mentioned characters, like others previously mentioned, represent the cavemen and their culture. An example of this is set in the following, where the description of Bacchus or Jesus is made into a tale in the entertainment of children. As can be seen, the word flesh was conveniently substituted for a variant, the word fleece,

> There comes a white swelling, or a bright (white) spot, reddish-white, **Lev 13: 19 (Genesis 25:25).**

> Mary (Jocasta) had a little Lamb (Oedipus), whose flesh (fleece) was white (leper) as snow.

> He whose locks (hair) are bound with gold (blond), Ruddy (red-skin) Bacchus, **Lore of Dionysus.**

The descriptions given above are explicit when narrating the appearance of the character in question. There should be no questions in the mind of the reader at this point. The red color of his skin is another symbol of the transparency mentioned in Leviticus.

The colors red (skin) and yellow/blond (hair) are the favorite colors of the Vatican, something they dramatized in the Pope's costume, when the Pope makes an appearance. This redness is because they lack the nectar (melanin), thus making their blood vessels visible, **Gen 25:25**.

Red (skin), yellow (hair): Pope's costume colors Bacchus' red skin is referred to as ruby-ish; hence the English word rub-bish. This redness is seen in albinos, due to blood vessels visible for the lack of pigment. Another related word to these historical findings, is the word shit. This word is the Hebrew pronunciation of the name Sat (Satan), or Seth.

Ruby-ish: Rubbish
Sat (Seth): Shit, Satan

The slang word caca is derived from the Latin word caecu (caucus), the same word from whence we derive the word Caucasian. The word feces on the other hand, learned its origin in the Egyptian word fikh (fig, fuck), the name of the oracle from whence the cavemen learned their knowledge of self.

Caecu (Cauc): Caca
Fikh (fig, fuck): Feces

The word fuck which appears also as a variant of the Egyptian word fikh is the result of Jesus' cursing of the fig tree or oracle, when the same refused to give him the knowledge of his fate. He vowed that no cavemen would learn from the tree thereafter, hence the phrase fuck you.

> Let no man eat (learn) from you hereafter (hence the phrase, fikh (fuck: fig) you), **Mathew 21: 19.**

Strangely, the word garbage is an adjective used to describe anything emanating from the west. The word gharb is Arabic meaning west. This word is later suffixed with the word age, bringing the same to identify the west or western world, the realm of the cavemen. The Spanish language derives the word garabato (junk, trashy) from this word.

Gharb: West
Gharb: Garb-age
Garb: Garabato (trashy)

Another word that should not go ignored is the word trash. This word is derived from the word Turk, from whence we get the name Turkey a country which carries the name of the fouled (field) animal from Noah's ark. This word originated in the Egyptian language, meaning to leave, to abandon, it is also seen in the Arabic language as tarak (track), also meaning to leave.

Turkh (Track): Trash, left behind in oblivion

Before the advent of the cavemen, there were no such thing as diversity; the other ethnic groups are the product of miscegenation between the two extremes, the Afrikoid and his Caucasoid counterpart.

The people of the cave had no idiom or language of their own; they brayed instead, **Job 30:6**. Upon their first contact with Egyptians as they left the cave, they could not understand the idiom and language of their hosts.

The Egyptians (Afrikans) used to refer to us (Greeks) as children, **Timaeus by Plato (Paul)**.

I write to you dear children, 1 **John 2:12**

The book is given to him who is not learned saying, read this, he says I'm not learned, **Isaiah 29:12**.

I do not know how to speak; I am only a child (cave dwellers), **Jeremiah 1:6**.

When I was a child a talked like a child, I thought like a child and I reasoned like a child, **Corinthians 13:11.**

After stealing the fire (knowledge), the cavemen became gods, knowing the knowledge of good and evil or science of opposites. They began to create their own version of masonry, a brotherhood known in the Egyptian language as "Sin-t", the Romans called it "Sinit", while other Caucasians called it "Senate".

The mass exodus of albinos from Egypt to the caves and wilderness is fore-told. They would return with a vengeance, hence Seven against Thebes. This determination to return is what Caucasians refer to as fari-dom (freedom), and means domain of enlightenment. This saga and their true origin are the great secrets held by the Masonic fraternity, it is the birth imprisonment and return of the cavemen from his environment. We can see in the Quran and the Bible that both, Jesus and Muhammad ordered secrecy.

I (Prometheus, Jesus) come as a thief…A thief does not come except to steal, kill and destroy, **Rev 16: 15; John 10: 10**.

They (cavemen, children) steal a hearing (fire, wisdom), **Quran 72**.

I open my mouth in riddles; I will reveal (give you the fire) things kept secret from the foundation of the world (Roman Empire)... See to it that no man knows it, **Matthew 13: 34; Matthew 9:3.**

You will hear the truth (about yourself), and the truth shall make you fire (enlightened: know thy self), **John 8: 32.**

Let no one identify you lest they stone (cave) you back to your (cave) culture, **Quran 18:19**.

According to the above instructions, the stolen knowledge is to be kept secret, and shared only among brothers in the lodge (temple).

The child grew and waxed strong... Filled with wisdom (god and evil). Esau (cavemen) was a cunning Hun (savage), He began to be mighty upon the earth, **Luke 2: 40; Genesis 25: 27; 1Chronicles 1: 10**.

He says: I am the light (Pied piper) of the world (world power)...as long as I'm in this world; I'm the ruler of the world, **John 9: 5; John 8: 5**.

The Lord (Aries: Aryan) is a man of war, who is able to make (declare) war with him? **Exodus 15: 3; Rev 13: 4.**

The history of the rise (and subsequent fall) of the cavemen is beginning to take shape. After being raised into full manhood, the child would return only to depose his father, the king. Remember, endogamy (incest) is what Oedipus practiced after killing his father, the king.

Go to the city with this paper currency (dollar) of

> yours; seek the purest food (best living standards) you can purchase with it, **Quran 18: 19.**

The science of opposites can be easily seen in the process of endogamy which brought about the albino (Homo erectus) race. Each generation became worse than the previous, this is the point made previously by Ms Hamilton.

> We created (made) manu in the best (genetic) essence then we de-gene-rated (degraded) him to the lowest, **Quran 95:4.**

In the same fashion in which scientists tamper with food today, the people of yore tampered with genetics seeking a specific product. The people practiced something endogamy or monarchy. One can remove the nutritional value from food, likewise one can remove the nectar (melanin) from the human body; Michael Jackson was living proof that such thing is possible.

They created a race of people who had to be sent to the cave to dwell therein, since they could not help being wicked. The word leper-atory is a phonetic variant of the word labor-atory, monumental evidence to these findings. Liber-atory: Leper-atory (laboratory), labra (leper).

The word leper is a phonetic deterioration of the word Liber, the Roman name of god Bacchus. This name is later attributed to the dog, the one who retrieved Romulus and Remus from the river Tiber, hence the name Liber-t-r retriever (Labrador retriever). The name Tiber is a variant of the word Thebes, the place of birth of the albino (Homo erectus). The dog-head is an icon of the Cain-ine (canine) people, known as Lycaon (Legion) or people of Thessaly.

> Tib- r: Tiber
> Tib-s: Thebes

The association of the words Liber-t-r and Labrador is by symbols, the Canaanite (canine) symbol and that of the albino people. The mother-dog in question is the jackal that raised Romulus and Remus, who by retrieving the twins gave birth to the title Labrador retriever. And thus began the phrase, Son-of-a-bitch: Romulus who killed his brother Remus (Cain and Abel), raised by a female dog, the Old Dame Dob

The dog symbol has a clear spot also in the story of Cain and Abel, an alternate version of Romulus and Remus. It is the name Cain that which gave us the word Cain-ine (canine). The dog that retrieved and raised Romulus and Remus is mentioned with some degree of subtlety in the Catholic religious culture of Mexico. This dog is called Guada-lupe, meaning dog-goddess.

Founding of the World

(Roman Empire: Re-biblic)

Let us (cavemen) build us a city (on a hill) whose top (power, greatness) may reach the heavens, **Gen 11:4**.

He sets his foundation on the holy mountain (The mountain of the Lord, Capitol hill), **Psalms 87:1.**

A city on a hill cannot be hidden, **Matthew 5: 14**.

The name of the city (world power) of my God (world leader) is New Jerusalem (New world order), **Revelation 3:12**.

You (cavemen) have been allowed (to build) this city, that which engenders (produces) it and that which it engenders (produces), **Quran 90: 1-2.**

In hoc signo vinces:
With this symbol you subdue, control.

The following is the oath of induction to the Jesuit order of the masons, the most powerful fraternity to date, under which come the Skull and Bones, Knights of Templar and others. The founding of the Roman Empire was founded on Masonic principles. All nations co-opted in the capitalist culture are based on the same tenets, Christianity/capitalism, the goal they all aspire under Caucasian leadership.

> I_______________, now in the presence of Almighty God, the blessed Virgin Mary, the blessed St. John the Baptist, the Holy Apostles, St. Peter and St. Paul, and all the saints, sacred host of Heaven, and to you, my Ghostly Father, the superior general of the Society of Jesus, founded by St. Ignatius Loyola, in the pontification of Paul the Third, and continued to the present, do by the womb of the Virgin, the matrix of God, and the rod of Jesus Christ, declare and swear that His Holiness, the Pope, is Christ's Vice-Regent and is the true and only head of the Catholic or Universal Church throughout the earth; and that by the virtue of the keys of binding and loosing given to His Holiness by my Savior, Jesus Christ, he hath power to depose heretical Kings, Princes, States, Commonwealths, and Governments, and they may be safely destroyed.
>
> Therefore to the utmost of my power I will defend this doctrine and His Holiness' right and custom against all usurpers of the heretical or Protestant authority whatever, especially the Lutheran Church of Germany, Holland, Denmark, Sweden and Norway, and the now pretended authority and Churches of England and Scotland, and the branches of same now established in Ireland and on the continent of America and elsewhere and all adherents in regard that they may be usurped and heretical, opposing the sacred Mother Church of Rome. I do now denounce and disown any allegiance as due to any heretical king, prince or State, named Protestant or Liberal, or obedience to any of their laws, magistrates or officers.
>
> I do further declare the doctrine of the Churches of England and Scotland of the Calvinists, Huguenots,

and others of the name of Protestants or Masons to be damnable, and they themselves to be damned who will not forsake the same. I do further declare that I will help, assist, and advise all or any of His Holiness's agents, in any place where I should be, in Switzerland, Germany, Holland, Ireland or America, or in any other kingdom or territory I shall come to, and do my utmost to extirpate the heretical Protestant or Masonic doctrines and to destroy all their pretended powers, legal or otherwise.

I do further promise and declare that, not withstanding, I am dispensed with to assume any religion heretical for the propagation of the Mother Church's interest; to keep secret and private all her agents' counsels from time to time, as they entrust me, and not to divulge, directly or indirectly, by word, writing or circumstances whatever; but to execute all that should be proposed, given in charge, or discovered unto me by you, my Ghostly Father, or any of this sacred order.

I do further promise and declare that I will have no opinion or will of my own or any mental reservation whatever, even as a corpse or cadaver, but will unhesitatingly obey each and every command that I may receive from my superiors in the militia of the Pope and of Jesus Christ. That I will go to any part (of the four corners) of the world whithersoever I may be sent, to the frozen regions north, jungles of India, to the centers of civilization of Europe, or to the wild haunts of the barbarous savages of America without murmuring or repining, and will be submissive in all things, whatsoever is communicated to me.

I do further promise and declare that I will, when opportunity presents, make and wage relentless war, secretly and openly, against all heretics, Protestants and Masons, as I am directed to do, to extirpate them from the face of the whole earth; and that I will spare neither age, sex nor condition, and that will hang, burn, waste, boil, flay, strangle, and bury alive these infamous heretics; rip up the stomachs and wombs of their women, and crush their infants' heads against the walls in order to annihilate their execrable race.

That when the same cannot be done openly I will secretly use the poisonous cup, the strangulation cord, the steel of the poniard, or the leaden bullet, regardless of the honor, rank, dignity or authority of the persons, whatever may be their condition in life, either public or private, as I at any time may be directed so to do by any agents of the Pope or Superior of the Brotherhood of the Holy Father of the Society of Jesus.

In confirmation of which I hereby dedicate my life, soul, and all corporal powers, and with the dagger which I now receive I will subscribe my name written in my blood in testimony thereof; and should I prove false, or weaken in my determination, may my brethren and fellow soldiers of the militia of the Pope cut off my hands and feet and my throat from ear to ear, my belly be opened and sulfur burned therein with all the punishment that can be inflicted upon me on earth, and my soul shall be tortured by demons in eternal hell forever (**Acts 1: 16-18**).

I will in voting always vote for a Knight of Columbus in preference to a Protestant, especially a Mason, and that I will leave my party so to do; that if two Catholics are on the ticket I will satisfy myself which is the better supporter of Mother Church and vote accordingly. I will not deal with or employ a Protestant if in my power to deal with or employ a Catholic. I will place Catholic girls in Protestant families that a weekly report may be made of the inner movements of the heretics.

> I will provide myself with arms and ammunition that I may be in readiness when the word is passed, or I am commanded to defend the Church either as an individual or with the militia of the Pope. All of which I,_______________, do swear by the blessed Trinity and blessed sacrament which I am now to receive to perform and on part to keep this my oath. In testimony hereof, I take this most holy and blessed sacrament of the Eucharist and witness the same further with my name written with the point of this dagger dipped in my own blood and seal in the face of this holy sacrament.

When John F. Kennedy was running for president of the United States, the subject of loyalty to the Pope or to America was brought to question. He made it clear that he will separate his church from his decision making. Based on the above, it is impossible to do so. He represents the same child who emanated from the cave only to kill his father and rule the world with a rod of iron. The child (cavemen) killed his father, and is therefore referred to in the hymnal as the Widow's son, **Luke 7:12**.

The child grew and became mighty on the land, opted to build an Empire that would reflect his resolve to control and later destroy the planet; an empire with which he lived a prodigal life. The city built would later be known as, the city on a hill, Capitol Hill that is. The city is also known as state or re-biblic (republic), and in children's tales it would be known as the house that Jack (Bacchus, Jesus) built.

Khan-Baal: Cannibal (Hannibal)

The child was later known as a mighty Khun (Hun, Hunter); an earlier form of the word khan-Baal (Cannibal). This name is later known as Hannibal or Khannibal. Those who believe Hannibal to be different from the Arabs of today are sadly mistaken. He may have been a strategic warrior, but he was still an Arab.

The time for the founding of a nation is nigh, the founding of the re-biblic (republic) of Rome is beginning to take shape. The compound word re-biblic is later pronounced re-public, the act of re-grouping people under the biblical concept. The rejoining of the cavemen under such banner came only after their dispersion (Diaspora), throughout the caves and deserts of Eur-Asia, **Genesis 11: 3**; **Job 30: 6**.

Biblic: Piblic (Public)

The establishment of a state was well on its way. It had to come, no matter the cost, as seen in the Jesuit oath read earlier. For this was the only way that the Caucasian race would be able to create an environment, or a state to derail the course (curse) Mother Nature set upon them.

The word state is derived from the name Sat (Seth), the very same word from whence we derive the word Satan. It is also the second word in the compound word khir-ast (Christ). This word is adopted into the English language as the superlative form est, i.e. high-est, great-est, m-est (most), etc. This word is also suffixed to some adjectives in order to denote proficiency, i. e. violinist, pharmacist, therapist, etc.

Ast/Sat (Seth): State

The child grew to be a mighty Hun (Hcinous), an Egyptian word meaning, ruthless, savage and wicked. No one dares challenge him in war. Most European countries were founded or ruled by these savage cavemen. The mighty Khun (Hun) describes Attila, founder of Hun-gary.

Attila: Founder of Hun-gary
Hun: Heinous (ruthless, savage, wicked

Hun-t: Hunter, a cunning one, **Gen 25:27**

The Brutus (British) isle was founded also by one of these heinous cavemen. The first British monarch was King Brutus (Brute), known to Greeks as, Menelaus. He is known in Biblical circles as Emanuel, a Cretan who migrated to what is now called the British Isles.

Brutus:
Greek Menelaus
Biblical Immanuel
Founder of Crete Britain (Great Britain)

Brutus (Menelaus, Immanuel) left the island of Crete and settled in the isles that today carry his name. He then called it Crete Brut-n (Britain), meaning, children of Cretan Brutus, but was pronounced later "Great" Britain.

Crete Brute-n: Great Britain

The afore-mentioned proves beyond a shadow of doubt that Caucasians are all of the same seed, the hue-less seed. The same role played by Menelaus (Brutus), in relation to the Trojan War, is the same role played by Brut-n (Britain) at the so-called World Wars.

Their act of re-grouping is called re-ligare (religion), a Latin word meaning, to re-attach, re-tie or re-group. This re-attachment or re-grouping is later called re-biblic, hence the phrase re-public. The re-tying or re-assemble these tribal families, is dramatized in the initiation into masonry. This re-ligare or re-binding is symbolized by a rope on their neck, called the cable tow (tie).

The wearing of the so-called neck-tie originated here. This re-attachment is symbolized by the Masonic rope called the cable tie (tow). Cable tie (tow): Symbolic of the re-assembly or re-ligare (re-attachment, re-bind) of the Caucasian race following their Diaspora in the caves of Europe and Asia.

> Let us build ourselves a city (on a hill), lest we remain scattered upon the face of the earth, **Gen 11: 4**.

> Hold tight to the rope (cable tow) of Al-la (the prince), and don't be divided, **Quran 3: 103**.

> If Satan (church) casts (separate from) out Satan (state), he is divided against himself, how then will his kingdom (capitalism, empire) stand? **Matt 12: 26.**

Re-ligare: Religion
Re-biblic: Republic

Now, it is clear that the companion of the cave founded a re-ligare (religion) in order to create the re-biblic (republic). This is the primary reason why church cannot be separated from state. The question is later addressed on the subject, by the founder himself (cavemen). The re-biblic (republic) came after the stealing of the knowledge of opposites (good and evil).

The beginning of the formation of such re-biblic (republic), is known today as New World Order, and is sometimes disguised under the euphemism global. The new world order is called New Testament, the philosophy for the new world.

New World
New Testament
New World Order (Globalism)

> New World Order (New Testament), one ruling race (monarchy), one culture, and one set of laws.

A political system was set up so that the corrupt leaders would be selected and would rule at will. This system is called capitalism, a Roman concept taken from the Biblical teachings. Capitalism is a word deriving from the Italian word Capo (head, captain). This word is derived from the Egyptian name Khu-Fu (Chief, Che-op), known as Jacob, Melkizedek, Aesculapius and Hippocrates, who is said to be the geneticist who designed the albino race.

The Bible refers to the Khu-fu (Capo) as king or lord, and the same kings (political), leaders or landlords decide and establish the rules governing all members of a society. The affluent members of society are called the capi, meaning the captains, chieftains. These heads of families would then select amongst themselves, the godhead or absolute leader, who would then be called Capo di capi, meaning Captain of captains, Lord of lords, King of kings, Holy of Holies, etc.

Religious fanatics have made gods of their leaders, as is mentioned in the hymnal (Bible). The Bible is the book of choice of the companions of the cave, the rise and fall of the Roman (cavemen) Empire. The major problem with the Bible is that the Caucasian race has glamorized this rise and fall.

> God stands in the congregation of the Mighty (Primus entre pares, world powers); He judges among the gods (heads of states), **Psalms 82:1**.

> He says: As long as I'm in the world, I am the light (rulers) of the world (Roman Empire), King of kings (Capo di capi), Lord of Lords (Holy of hollies), **John 9: 5; Rev 17:14**.

The system of selection mentioned above, is also the practice used at the Vatican to select the Pope. It is the same used by the Mafia to select the godhead among Mafia families. In the United States, this system is referred to as Electoral

Colleague, erroneously pronounced college. This group is the one in-charge of selecting the president according to his popularity with the people.

The author of this book maintains that there has never been a man named Jesus who walked the earth, and doing the supernatural things attributed to him. As is typical among Caucasians, the story has been glamorized and sensationalized to evoke sympathy.

The Cavemen seem to take great pleasure in self deceit. Why the lies? The lies are for world racial superiority, and nothing else. They have glamorized their expulsion from Egypt with a religious tale called Exodus, the story of the albino (hybrid or Hebrew) exiled from Thebes (Egypt).

World racial superiority is manifested in an ideology Caucasians call monarchy, meaning one race, one god, one ideology, etc. The concept of monarchy is the only way Caucasians can produce Caucasians, a defective or recessive gene.

The phrase e pluribus Unum engraved on the United States one (1) dollar bill attests to the afore-said. <u>E pluribus Unum: Out of many (races), one (ruling)</u>. The ruling class will dictate its will to the rest of the components of the "human" family. This is evident in all areas of the planet to which the Caucasian reaches; they take charge of everything and everyone.

Subdue the land, **Gen 1: 28**

I came, I saw, I subdued, **Julius the Czeu-r.**

The subduing of the people on the land is well documented afore-hand on the United States one (1) dollar bill. The same has inscribed on it the phrase annuit coeptis, meaning our endeavor (task). This is no coincidence; it is a very detailed and elaborate plan for world domination (demonation) and supremacy, Annuit Coeptis: Our conspiracy (task).

The higher you ascend the mountain, the farther (more wisdom) you can see (learn); go tell (reveal) it on the mountain (at Patmos island). This is the symbol of the mountain upon which Jesus is alleged to have taken the disciples in order to reveal to them the stolen knowledge, the book of Revelation. It is the hill upon which the city is build, known in contemporary culture as Capitol Hill, **Matthew 5: 14.**

This mountain is also the one upon which Jesus appointed the eleven disciples who were later converted into swoon (Legion). When they learned about the nature of self, they symbolically became swoon or pigs. When the pig became their national (official) symbol, the flesh of the pig became forbidden food.

Jesus is nothing but the character used by the writers of the Bible to represent the Caucasian race as a whole. His story carries many different names, all of which are variations in characteristics of the Caucasian race, Oedipus is one such story. The son of the king, the prince, came to seize the kingdom from his father. The cycle of the lion is similar to that of the saga of the cavemen, hence the phrase lion of Yeti (Jedi: Juda).

The people of Jedi (Juda) are called the lion of Jedi (Juda) for specific reasons. The life cycle of the lion is, as the lion is sent to live in the wilderness (cave), he grows and become experienced and strong. He then returns to the pride only to dethrone the reigning lion, usually his father.

Yeti (Jedi): Juda

Once the father is gone, the lion then destroys his father's brood and mates with his own mother (mother fucker). This process is known as endogamy, incest and/or monarchy. The first ever recorded literary story of such lion (of Juda) is known as Oedipus Rex. The word Yeti (Jedi, Juda) became the word Yetish (Yiddish), the mother of the Hebrew (hybrid) language. The albinos exiled from Egypt are the first hybrid (Hebrew) the world has ever seen.

Yeti: Yetish (Yiddish)

The Hebrew owns that version of the Bible which deify their culture, while the Christian owns that version of the same which deify their culture. Both groups are from the same lineage, genetically speaking, **John 4:7**. The elder brother refuses to accept his younger brother, remember, Jesus claims to come only for the Hebrew (Jew). The Good Samaritan woman calls him a Czeu (Jew), and then his followers refer to him as son of King David.

> Have mercy on me o son of David (Jesus or Solomon?), **Matt 15: 22.**

> I was sent <u>only</u> (for Jews) to the lost sheep (field animal) of the house of Israel (cavemen), **Matthew 15: 24**.

> How is it that you (cavemen) being a Czeu (Jew), ask a drink from me, a Samaritan (Old dame Dob)? **John 4:9.**

> Let the children of Israel (cavemen) know that God made that Jesus (from albino, dead, mortal), whom you crucified (rejected and placed in the cave), **Acts 2: 36.**

Racism is the meaning behind the question asked to Jesus by the Samaritan woman. The question implies that the Jews are not to help the Samaritans and vice-versa. Then, to confirm such racism, Jesus told many before and after the woman, that he came only for a certain ethnic group, the Czeu (Jew) or children of Israel.

The afore-mentioned quote says that Jesus was sent to the cavemen, known also as children (of Israel). The quote that follows says that these children (cavemen) executed him, yet these get offended when they are reminded of that. Then the Christian fool has the audacity to suggest that the Jew is elect of God. What is even worse; why not follow Judaism if the elect of God are the Jews? Why is Jesus teaching Christianity and not Judaism?

The belief that the Czeu (Jew) is the elect or favorite of God has permeated the biblical philosophy in its entirety, yet they are said to have murdered Jesus, one of their own. The

Good Samaritan, about whom we read previously, is a female. Though some versions portray this Samaritan as male, the original Good Samaritan was female. This story does not end there, and continues with the drunk (wounded) Jesus being put on a donkey, since he could not find his way home.

> Your King (of kings) is coming to you meek (lowly, humiliated, disgraced), on a duncey (donkey), **Matthew 21:5.**

The donkey, on which Jesus is put and sent home by the Good Samaritan, represents ignorance. In fact, the word donkey is a variant of the word dunce, a cavemen's trait. The word monkey on the other hand, a derivative of the word monk, describes the cavemen. This word evolved from his ape-like form of life in the cave. The word monk is derived from the Egyptian words Mun (manu), meaning, cavemen and khi, meaning conscience.

> Dunce: Duncey (donkey)
> Mun-kh: Monk (monkey, ape-man)

It is very amazing to see the length to which Caucasians will go in order to conceal the truth, **John 8: 30**. Religion is nothing but the glamorization of the Caucasian saga, his birth (hybrid) and hiber-nation (Hebrew-nation) into the cave. One can now see clearly that, Jesus doesn't only represent the Caucasian lineage, but he is also of Caucasian idiosyncrasy.

Have you wondered why is it that he tells his people that they must pay debt (debit: tax). The words debt, debit and dve (due), are all evolved from the name Davd (Daud), his father, symbolically speaking.

Devd (debit or tax) is instituted by the Caucasian race, in order to loot and pillage those people he did not murder in his murderous rampage on his quest for racial superiority. Every culture has a name for their king. Jews call him king, Egyptians call him Pharaoh, Romans call him Caesar, Japanese call him Emperor, and British call him Lord or Majesty, and so on.

> If anyone wants to sue you and take away your tunic, let him have your cloak also, **Matt 5: 40.**

> Render to Czeu-r the things that are Czeu-r's, **Matt 22: 21.**

The original name for the so-called tax is debt (davit), in honor of David, the king. Jesus the crook, of whom no one wants to talk, is one of the many personifications of the cavemen. Christian religious fanatics have failed to ask the most important question. Why was Jesus crucified in the company of two thieves?

> Tau-t (Davd): David, debit, debt

The answer can be found in aforementioned quotes and in the story of Prometheus, he is the thief who stole the fire (wisdom, revelation) and gave it to Manu (men). Jesus represents the same character represented by Prometheus, Socrates, Santa Claus and the other characters.

Go to the city with your paper currency (money), seek with it the highest living standard, make sure no one recognizes you, lest they stone (cave) you back to your culture, **Quran 18: 19.**

The thief that Jesus is can be understood when he tells his people that they should pay their taxes. The word tax is from the Egyptian word tukh (dog), meaning to take, seize, steal, etc. The words dog and thug are derivations of this word.

Tukh: Take, tax, touch, thug, dog

The saying in the above ending quote says that you should also; let him have your cloak along with your tunic. This does not mean that Jesus ever uttered such thing; it merely suggests or means that the culture called Christianity sees things in that light.

The word credit, antonym of the word debit, has its origin also in the religious jargon. The word credit is a variant of the word creed, and is from the Greek word kretus, meaning belief. The Greeks in turn, learned it from the Egyptian word khir-t, the first part of the word khir-ast (Christ).

Credo (creed): Credit

Something that needs to be made clear is that, when Jesus speaks, he is only echoing the tenets of Caucasian societies, nature and culture. Jesus never existed; he represents the placement and escape from the cave, the rise and fall of the

Caucasian (cavemen) empire. The entire English language is the result of a Caucasian imposed racist and religious dialect.

The character name Jesus then tells you that, don't only pay taxes, but give up your all. We must remember that the kingdom (empire, culture) for which people gave their lives, must remain ours, **Revelation 3:11**.

We cannot over-look the Cain's contribution to this orgy of words and concepts, which gave formation to the phallic culture. Like Jesus and the other characters, he is only a personage who represents an ethnic group and its social concepts. The word gain is a direct result of the name and the concept of Cain, who by other accounts is the prodigal son.

Cain: Gain

The prodigal (opulent) son took the share of his father's (patria) wealth, with which he created the city on a hill. The word profit is the direct result of the word prophet, all of which is also religious in nature, for the re-biblic (republic).

The aforementioned information may seem like a coincidence, we must abandon that silly belief; nothing in a capitalist culture is left to chance. The organizers, protractors and promoters of religion have calculated everything.

Prophet: Profit

Bear in mind that the story is a metaphor, the god of war. War is declared on the King (father) only after the prince returns (resurrects) from the cave, **Matthew 22:13**.

The belief that Caucasians have the right to the world's resources may have been triggered by their myth-understanding or misunderstanding of this Biblical concept. Capitalism or Christianity is nothing but a large scale business; this explains the biblical narrative of Jesus expelling the merchants from the temple. The resources are the result of the feats and loot of war.

> Their princes were brighter than snow (Caucasians), whiter than milk, their body more ruddy (red) than rubies, **Lamentations 4:7.**

> How have you fallen oh Lucifer? Is this the **man** (God of war, Exodus 15: 3) that made nations tremble? **Isaiah 14:16.**

Lucifer, as Buri is also known, is the most feared of the four seasonal winds, of the four posted at the four corners of the world. He caused awesome fear in the hearts of men. Buri is the son of Amir (Ymir) in Nors literature, he is the abominable snowman.

There are many letters of the alphabet that often substituted each other throughout Caucasian linguistic history, they are, **C, G, J, H, K, Q, X** and **Y**. This is the reason it has become very difficult to trace the origin of some words.

The battle for the rest of the world's resources, promises to be fierce and very deadly, Caucasians refer to it as feudalism. This war is known as **WWI** and **WWII**; and is only a continuation of that which began as the cavemen left the cave. The Lord of war mentioned above, is god Aries, known to Romans as Mars. The word March, as one sets out for war, is an invocation of this war-god. March (Aries)**:** Invocation of god Mars (March) as the soldiers head for war.

God Mars or Aries is from whose name the war-mongers derive the title Arie-n (Aryan). Another title evolving from this god is the title Aries-t-khart, better known as the Aristocrat. The cavemen community is devoted to this god and his principles, no matter their religious persuasion.

> When you are about to go into battle, the priest

(learned) shall come forward and address the army, **Deuteronomy 20: 2.**

You may cut down trees that you know are not fruit trees and use them to build siege works until the city (of Troy) at war with you falls, **Deuteronomy 20:20.**

Prepare for battle against her! Arise let us attack at noon, **Jeremiah 6:4.**

Alas, how strange is it that we are preparing to commit great sinful acts; driven by the desire to enjoy royal happiness (elitism, kingdom), we are bent on killing our own relatives (feudalism), **Bhagavad Gita 1:44.**

If I must slay (murder) the joy of my house, my daughter, a father's hands stained with dark streams, flowing from blood of a girl slaughtered before the altar...

And all her prayers-cries of Father, Father, her maiden life, these they held as nothing...

He (Agamemnon) dared the deed slaying his child to help a war, **The war for Troy.**

War broke out in (the kingdom of) haven (elite). The kingdom of have-n (opulence) suffers violence, and the (most) violent will take it by force, **Matthew 11: 12.**

The son (Zeus) and his angels (Olympians) fought, **Rev 12: 7.**

The king (Chronis) and his angels (Titans) fought, **Rev 12: 7.**

His (Caucasian) rule (policy) extends from sea to sea and from the River (beginning) to the ends of the earth, **Zechariah 9:10.**

The war by now had reached Olympus-the gods were ranged against each other... The other gods were now fighting, too, as hotly as the men, and Zeus sitting apart in Olympus laughed pleasantly to him-self when he saw god matched against god. **Edith Hamilton, 1940.**

The Baghavad Gita, the Krishna's sacred text, relates a similar story of war for wealth (kingdom) among family members, again, known as family feud The problem with religious and dogma, is that its adherents believe themselves to have a monopoly on wisdom (knowledge).

Not so strange is the fact that the aforementioned war is deified in the Krishna culture. Lord Krishna, the god of war **(Exodus 15: 3)**, orders Arjuna (his messenger) to slay his family and get the kingdom. This is family feud, whether or not accepted by religious fanatics.

Agamemnon then agonizes over the sacrifice of one of his relatives, his own daughter. Agamemnon (Arjuna?) sends for his daughter with the promise of marriage to Aquilles, she found out later that she was headed to her funeral, not her marriage. As much as she pleaded, her clamor fell on deaf ears. I submit to you, the reader, that the story is the same; Agamemnon is the Greek version of the Indian Arjuna.

The story you are now reading, is reminiscent of Abraham, who was resigned to sacrifice his then only son, Ishmael. This sacrifice is the killing of the youngsters on the field of battle in order to conquer territory and so expand the kingdom (empire).

The aforementioned war is very popular in most cultures and has caused a tremendous impact in the literary arena.

This great family feud is known in Caucasian culture as the battle of Troy; Arab culture knows it as the battle of Badr; and the Indian (India) culture knows it as the battle of Kuruk. The family feud is known to the Czeus (Jews) as the war of Jerusalem, **Rev 3: 12**.

The above mentioned war is eloquently narrated in the books of Judges and Samuel. Caucasians are all a single family, whether they are Czeus (Jews), Christians, Muslims, Zoroaster, Buddhist, etc. This has created a sense of monarchy among its followers.

Battle of Troy: Greek literature
Battle of Badr: Arabic literature
Battle of Kuruk: Krishna literature
Battle of Jerusalem: Hebrew literature

The central theme in the above mentioned battle is the handing over of the family wealth to new generations of family members. This happens upon the child's return from exile imposed by his father, the King. Now that the son is back, he will take the kingdom (opulence, wealth) away from his father who is in haven (opulence, elitism), **Matthew 11: 12.**

The great battle of the kin, or family feud as it is better known, is documented in the annals of history as Feudalism. This war is, again, for control of the world's resources (kingdom). The word feud is of Egyptian origin, derived from the word faut, meaning law, rule, order, etc, hence the new world Order.

The family feud for the heavenly kingdom is as old as the Caucasian race, no matter the religious denomination. Zeus (Caucasian) is the God-head or God among gods (world powers), he judges among the gods, mentioned in book of **Job 82: 1.**

Faut (Feud): Fait (Fight: veto, veda)
Feudalism: World wars, family conflicts
Families: Hapsberg, Dupont, Getty,
Rockefeller, Rothchilds,etc

Any culture that encourages the conquering and pilfering of the world resources should be carefully examined. The reason he (cavemen) encourages this war, is in order to establish him-self king or owner of these resources. The war in it-self is caused by the greed inherent in the Caucasian race, **Romans 1: 29 - 31**.

Subsequent religions that stem from this war are a glamorization and deification of this capitalism or of the culture, established by warmongers, **Matthew 10: 35.**

The nature of the central characters of the above narrative is the subject of the book titled The Iceman Inheritance, by Michael Bradley. Mister Bradley attributes the cold blooded nature of the Caucasian, to his arctic environment. The above is a guaranty that the wealth will always be in the same race or family circle, a policy called monarchy. This is the case in the battles we have come to know as World Wars; the world in question is the Roman Empire.

The spirit of monarchy is a reminder of the ruthless and wicked nature of Capitalism (Christianity). The new lion king proceeds to erase all traces of the previous lion king; he kills the children of the previous king, his own family, brothers, sisters and all. In a capitalist society the woman much like the slave, she is only an addition to the king's assets; and a pawn in the strategy to preserve the kingdom; this is seen in the sacrifice of his daughter by Agamemnon.

Cavemen culture once believed that the sun rotated around the earth, and that the earth was a flat surface from which one would fall if he/she wandered far-off. They later learned that they were on the opposite side of wisdom. Likewise they believe the arrogant white male to be the central theme in society, only to be wrong again. Their heavenly father is Czeus, known by many other names. He is the main character in the concept of good and evil, and the prayer our father or father-lis (federal) system.

The concept of heaven and hell is nothing but a misconception the cavemen held concerning the science of opposites, or as they put it, the knowledge of good and evil. The name Eve, their symbolic mother, is from whence Caucasians produced the word Eve-il (evil).

It's worth mentioning, that the word haven is derived from the Egyptian word haf-n, meaning possession, enjoyment and pleasure. The kingdom of haven is anything that offers us opulence, joy and pleasure.

> Haf-n (haven): Opulence, possession, enjoyment and pleasure.

The word haven is nothing but the place where the gods (elite) dwell, it is also known as the hall of the elite (gods). The capital city of Havana, Cuba learns its name from here.

> Once upon a time there was a child who was punished by his parents because of bad behavior, among other things. The child was grounded in his bedroom for a period of time. Sitting idly in his bed, the he concocted a story of two imaginary friends, who dwell along with him in the bed-room. The one lives in the upper part of his closet, while the second lives in the bottom portion underneath his bed.
>
> Upon lifting his punishment, the parents called the child for supper. While having supper with his parents, the child narrates the story of his two imaginary friends to both of his parents. They found this behavior a bit peculiar and in turn, took the child to a psychologist.

After explaining his plight to the psychologist, the parents awaited his response. The psychologist then responded to the parents telling them that the child's behavior is very normal, and that they should occasionally play along the game with the child.

The above analogy is exactly what happened between the Caucasian and his Egyptian parents; he was punished in the cave for bad behavior, among other things. Subsequently he returns from his punishment (the cave), with a religion or culture which varies in name from time to time and place to place.

The imaginary friend living in the upper area of the closet is Dav-id the Dev-ine (God*)*; while the imaginary friend living below his bed, is the Diablo (Double, DeviI, Satan). Double because he is made in the mirror image and likeness of his maker. Organized religion is a figment of Caucasian imagination and nothing else, the Devine (Davd: God-head) and Dev-il (evil friend).

Expansion of Re-biblic

(Republic) Roman Empire

Have domino (domain) over the birds in the air, the fish in the sea, subdue the land, **Gen 1: 28**.

Ye (cavemen) are the light (leaders) of the world; let your light (policies, culture) shine (be disseminated) among Manu (men), **John 5: 16.**

The sons of God are summoned, and Satan (descendants of Seth) came among them, He was asked: Where have you been o Satan (descendants of Seth)? He responds, Rome-ing (roaming) and oscillating the earth, **Job 1: 6**.

You travel the land and sea seeking one proselyte (religious/political convert), when he is converted he is twice the hell child of you are, **Matthew 23: 15.**

The above quotes are but a literary narrative of current, passed events, current events and events to come. There is nothing supernatural or some hidden secret for which one needs special knowledge to de-code. The key to the understanding of literature is the exclusion of cathartic emotional and dramatic episodes.

The dissemination of the culture among Manu (men) is seen as Prometheus gives the fire (knowledge) to Manu (men).

This giving of fire (knowledge) is also dramatized as Santa Claus gives toys to children; it is the reason Jesus (Socrates) solicited the presence of children and was subsequently put to death.

The above quote gives us a clear understanding of the story of the Pied Piper, the man who delighted the rats with his sweet music and good intention, thus leading them down the road of perdition. The Pied Piper story is, like the others a metaphor. The word Pied is unique because it also means Piebald or melting pot. The Pied-piper leader or light of the world, **Matthew 5:14**; **Rev 17: 15.**

The expansion of the re-biblic (republic), or as we know it, the Roman Empire, is of extreme priority. Prometheus (Caucasian race) stole the fire (wisdom), only to give it to Manu (men), in the form of religious and political propaganda. The robbery of this knowledge is called stealing of a hearing in the Quran, the Islamic sacred text. The manner, in which this propagation took place, is narrated in the Christian (capitalist) hymnal as can be seen below.

> The waters you saw, upon which the Horae (w-hore) sits, are (a symbol of) people, multitude of nations and tongues (languages), **Revelation 17: 15**.

> The day of Pentecost had fully come; they (proselytes) were all with one accord in one place. They were filled with the Holy host and began to speak in (their native) tongues, **Acts 2: 1, 4.**

When this occurred, the multitude came together, were confused (melted pot), because everyone heard them (cavemen) speak in his own (native) language. How is it that we hear, each in our own (native) tongue (language) in which we were born? **Acts 2: 6, 8.**

The dissemination of the capitalist culture is the central theme in that which follows, the lands conquered by this culture.

> (From) The lands of Lydia (Asia Minor) rich in gold, of Phrygia (Asia west, Turkey) too…
>
> The sun-struck plains of Persia (Iran), the great walls of Bactria (Indo-European Iran)…
>
> The storm-swept country of the Medes (Mediterranean); and Arabia the Blessed, (To the rest of the world), **Lore of Dionysus/Bacchus.**

The aforementioned quotes are narratives of the dissemination of Caucasian culture (capitalism), each ethnic group or race assimilated the same in its native language. Each is to have a group that represents them at the place where they congregate, the place where the great Horae (whore) sits, the New York Bay. This melting pot of pluralism (nations and tribes) is a clear case of confusion.

> Con: With, jointly, together, mutuality.
> Fusion: Union, mixture, merger, combination, Amalgamation (melting pot)

It must be made clear to the reader that the words con-fusion is a compound meaning amalgamation, in other words, pluralism (melting pot). The compound word con-fusion means to blend-in together as one, hence the phrase melting pot. This melting pot as it is called will have one ruling race or class, the cavemen or Caucasian race, the governing laws will all be according to his nature, hence the phallic culture.

Following its expansion to neighboring regions, the Roman Re-biblic (republic) would then be brought to the Americas as the New Testament, the philosophical manual for the New World Order. Another name by which this dissemination is known is the Last Supper. Its original name is Bakh-Nakh (Pic-Nic), meaning good and evil; a phrase most famously known as Pic-Nic (Pic: Death, Nic: Life).

> Bakh: Pic (Good, alpha)
> Nikh : Nic (Evil, omega)

The above explains the similitude in the many capitalist religious ideologies that to this day has plague the earth. All cultures learned the knowledge, and interpret the same differently; this is according to race and regional factors as well. The most corrupt interpretation came as usual, from the cavemen. The pic-nic or Last Supper is the central them in the story of king Arthur and the Knights (learned men) of the Round table, the kingdom is called Camelot.

Camelot is the Kingdom of haven, King Arthur and the twelve (12) Knights (learned) of the Round (discus) table is the British version the Last Supper. The word knight is a visibly clear variant of the word know-ledge. Caucasian went on to teach the knowledge as Judaism and Christianity, the Arabs went on to teach it as Islam, the Persians teach it as Zoroastrianism, while in other areas of Asia it was thought as Buddhism, the Indian (of India) went on to teach it as Krishna, everyone in his own culture and tongue (native language).

The Caucasian and the Arab had the worst of all teaching methods; they did it by the sword. They call it Zionism and Crusade, the Arabs called theirs Jihad. They taught and did everything with the sword; the sword is the symbol of war, the wicked two-edged sword.

> I (Christianity, capitalism) did not come to bring peace, but a sword (war), **Matthew 10:34**.

> I (capitalism, Christianity) come as a thief, **Rev 16:15**.

> These things said He who has the sharp two-edge (alpha and omega) sword, **Rev 2: 12.**

The two-edge sword is the sword is known in Roman literature as "two-edged hatchet", used to split god Zeus' head in two parts giving birth to Athena. The Twin-Towers destroyed on September 11, 2001, were monuments to this two-edge sword, the science of good and evil or science of opposites, known also as two-lights (twilight). Their Christian culture, like that of the Arabs and the Hebrews, is disseminated through war.

The picnic or science of opposites is also the subject in the opening of the Quran, the Islamic sacred text. The Arab culture has translated the same as beneficent and merciful. There is a chapter dedicated to the science of opposites, this chapter is number fifty-five (55) and is name the Mercy. The Quran starts every chapter by saying:

> In the name of Al-la (the prince, the god), the rah-maan (alpha), (and) the rah-iym (omega)…

> He (prince) taught the two sciences (good and evil). He taught him (manu) the separation of the two (light and darkness)…

> He raised the have-n (opulence, elitism) and established balance (between two), **Quran 55.**

The battle for world superiority becomes fierce; the violent will take it by force, **Matthew 11: 12**, it is dramatized in the ritual we have come to know as baseball. In this drama, the child sets out to conquer the four corners of the world after dethroning his father, the king.

> In and around (domestic and international) the empire (kingdom), were four living creatures, **Rev 4: 6**.

> The four creatures (north, west, south and east) were full of eyes (espionage agencies) around (international) and within (domestic), **Rev 4: 8.**

> He cast him (cavemen) into the pit (cave), and shut him up and set a seal on him (in the cave), so that he should not deceive the four corners (north, west, south and east) of the earth, **Rev 20: 3**.

> But after these things he (cavemen) must be released (resurrection) for a little while. He will go out to deceive the nations, **Rev 20: 8.**

The four poles representing the corners of the world are known also to be the four children of Nikh-t, the cave goddess. Their names are Urb/Rub, (Arab and Europe), Mur (Moor, Amorite), Hypnos (hypnosis) and Somnus (sleep).

The four corners of the earth are known in the Christian culture as Matthew, Mark, Luke and John. These four echo the same events surrounding capitalism and communism; they are the four bases in the ritual (game) baseball. It is important to remember that capitalism and communism are two opposite sides of the very same coin, as are the democrat and republican parties.

The four creatures reining each in its own corner of the earth are also known to Greeks as the gods of the four winds, spring, summer, fall and winter. Argus is the god of many eyes, patron saint of the ship piloted by Jason and the Argo-nauts.

He is represented by the peacock whose tail symbolizes many the eyes (spies) on the world, **Rev 4: 8.**

Buri (Boreas): god of the north (arctic) wind, whose name is, evolved from the name Buri, son of Ymir (Amir) the abominable snowman, hence the north (home base). Romans call him Aquila (Eagle).

Khafir (Zephyr): God of the west wind, known as the first base in the dramatic ritual called baseball, made into a pass-time Romans call him Favonius (Lion).

Nut (Notus): God of the south wind, known as the second base in the dramatic baseball ritual. Romans call him Auster (Austerity).

Ur (Ares, Eros, Euro): God of the east wind, known as third base in the dramatic baseball ritual. Latin (Romans) calls him by the same name, Eurus (Euro).

The above-mentioned quotes are indicative of the Caucasian's rampage on the earth, following his release from the cave. This episode of the Caucasian saga is dramatized in the epic called Jason and the Argonauts. God Argus is the god possessing many eyes, and is symbolized by the peacock's tail (many eyes). He is the patron Argentina, South America, and also the patron saint of the city of Aragon (Oregon), in Spain.

The Islamic version is represented by Umar, Abu Bakr, Othman and Ali, known as Muhammad's faithful companions. Capitalism (monotheism) by any name is still the same. The four individuals representing the four corners of the planet under Caucasian control are sometimes referred to in masonry as the square. Greek literature knows these four as the four gods of the winds. They were once the protagonists in the children's tale known as the Fantastic four and D'artagnan and the Three Musketeers.

The four character mentioned later became Goldilocks and the Three bears, then the Wolf and the Three pigs and Dorothy the tin man, the lion and the Scarecrow in the story Wizard of Oz. Strangely, they are also seen in the hymnal (Bible) where Jesus is the fourth, as he travel to the heart of the earth were he claim to have seen three unclean spirits.

These four characters are also seen in the Krishna culture as the four Vedas. Each represents a pillar of the culture that is supposed to be established on the four corners of the earth. They must let their light (stolen knowledge) shine (be disseminated) among Manu (man).

Christian	Islamic	Greek	Krishna
John	Ali	Hypnus	Rig
Luke	Omar	Somnus	Sama
Mark	Abu Bakr	Urb/Rub	Yajur
Matthew	Othman	Mur/Amur	Atarva

The image here is goddess Nikht (night), she is the mother of Somnus, Buri, Urb and Hypnus

The information herein is available for those who want to do their homework. Religion and politics are very dangerous subjects; they seek absolute submission, subjection and servitude from their prey. Religious idiosyncrasy (theory) is political ideology (practice). These four are also known as the four horsemen of death or apocalypse.

> Behold a white hearse (horse), **Rev 6:2**.
>
> Behold a red hearse (horse), **Rev 6: 4.**
>
> Behold a black hearse (horse), **Rev 6:5**
>
> Behold a pale hearse (horse), **Rev 6:8**.

The first chariot had red horses, the second black, the third white and the fourth dappled... The one with the black hearses (horses) is going toward the north, the one with the white hearses (horses) toward the west, the one with the dappled hearses (horses) toward the south, **Zechariah 6:1, 5**.

> After this, I saw four angels (of death) standing at the four corners of the earth, holding back the four winds (of destruction) of the earth, **Rev 7:1**.
>
> Satan (descendants of Set) will be released from his prison (cave) and will go out to deceive the nations in the four corners (north, west, east and south) of the earth, **Rev 20:7**.
>
> To these four young men (Matthew, Mark, Luke and John) God (world leader, Pope) gave knowledge and understanding of all kind of literature (Christianity,

Islam, Judaism, Budhism, Krishna, Zoroastranism, etc) **Daniel 1:17**.

These are the four spirits of heaven (capitalism), going out from standing in the presence of the Lord (world leader, Pope), **Zechariah 6:5**.

Make a horn at each of the four corners (of the world), so that the horns (policies) and the altar (cultural values) are of one piece (the same), **Exodus 27: 2**.

There before me were four horns, **Zechariah 1:18.**

These four creatures reappear under separate and distinct icons, seen in **Rev 4: 7.**

Four great beasts each different from the others, came up out of the sea, **Daniel 7:2**.

I have scattered you the four winds of haven (heaven), **Zechariah 2:6**.

The eagle (bald) represents the current world power; this eagle sits on the mountain-top (Capitol Hill), from whence it sees the world and seizes world resources at will. The ritual of baseball is the best dramatization of this event.

The drama continues to become more and more interesting. The child managed to deceive the world with a philosophy called Christianity (capitalism). This cultural philosophy is the cavemen's best shot yet, convincing the world that he (devil) does not exist.

Following the conquest of the east, third base, the cavemen would have completed his annuit coeptis (mission). The (middle) east however, has proven a very formidable task. The battle of the east corner of the planet is the drama of the fight Cain (Caucasian) sustains with his brother Abel (Arab), before the murder.

The Arabs and the Europeans are family members; their kinship is shown in the story called Abraham and his wife Sara, known to Greeks as Philemon and his wife Baucis. The Caucasian race came from Abraham via Sara, while the Arab race came from Abraham via Hagar. Philemon is also the name of one of the many books of the hymnal (Bible).

The Caucasian trickster alleges that he is the favorite son of Abraham, due to an aborted attempt of Abraham to sacrifice his son Isaac. The concept is ridiculous at best; lie at worst, since Isaac at no time was ever Abraham's only son. The sacrifice of Abraham's only son is featured by Ishmael; since he is fourteen years Isaac's senior and was Abraham's only son for fourteen years.

> Abram was eighty-six (86) years old when Hagar bore Ishmael, **Genesis 16:16**.

> Now, Abraham was one hundred (100) years old when his son Isaac (swine) was born, **Genesis 21: 5.**

Another lie extant in the story of the Caucasian is the name Semitic (Simian). The adjective Semitic (Simian) is derived from the name Sam, Noah's first son and brother to Ham, Noah's second son. The Arabs are Simian (Semitic), while the Caucasians are Hamitic (Boers, boars, swine, Hebrews, etc).

The story of Cain and Abel, Romulus and Remus are but alternate versions of the sons of Noah and Abraham. The story of Noah is an older version of Abraham. The names Abra (boar, Iberia) ham (pig) are variants of the word boar, the wild pig, remember Ishmael is a wild man.

> He made them into **apes** (Arab icon) and **swoon** (Caucasian icon), **Quran 5:60.**

The word swoon is the plural form of the word swine. The difference between the Muslim Quran and the Christian Bible is the clarity and organization in which the riddles (parables) are written.

Swine: Singular
Swoon: Plural form

Caucasians and Arabs have exploited the naiveté of a multitude (mass) in complete and utter darkness (ignorance), after sending these people into mayhem. This ignorance, in which the people find themselves, is the brain-child of the Caucasian himself.

The Bible and Quran are historical accounts told in metaphorical (literary) or poetical form. Each of the previous mentioned cultures are in a race to prove its cultural superiority, hence organized religion. You have now that the Buddhists and the Krishna cultures are the counterparts of the violence created by the Caucasians and Arabs. Buddhist and Krishna cultures are in a heated race to each establish its own as the superior, under the banner of spiritualism.

Following the victory, in this family feud, the child (cavemen) established what we now know as Rome (New Jerusalem, New World Order, Babylon, etc), **Rev 3:12.**

The Hebrew culture is the same as the Christian culture, Caucasian world superiority. They say that Cain established Ankh (New Jerusalem, New World Order) after the murder of his brother, one of the Biblical names for Cain's son or new world is Ankh (Enoch). This word is a variant of the antonyms "nakh (life)" and "nikh (death)" **Gen 4: 17.**

Rome-ulus (Cain) rose-up against Remus (Abel), his brother and killed him, **Gen 4:8**.

> Rome-ulus (Cain) knew his wife and he built a city (Rome, Nod), **Gen 4: 17.**

> A city (Rome) set on a (Capitol) hill cannot be hidden, **Matt 5: 14.**

Not every nation welcomes Caucasian culture, there are those as we can see, hate cavemen culture with justified passion. Like the Krishna, the Hebrew and the Arab, the Caucasian claims his culture to be the world's savior.

There is a controversial nature in the very essence of the companions of the cave. They teach a very sophisticated form of anarchy they label fari-dome (freedom). The natural order of the world has been traded by the Caucasian race for the new world order. Then there are those who want nothing at all to do with Caucasian religious (political) ideology.

> They (mass, multitude) began to plead with him to depart their region (country), **Mark 5:17.**

> Others mocking said, they must be full of that <u>new</u> (world order) wine, **Acts 2:13**.

> Harlotry, wine (Old Testament), and the <u>new</u> wine (New Testament) enslave the heart, **Hosea 4: 11**.

Strangely enough, the word n-rkh (anarchy) is a negation of the Albinos (Homo erectus), progenitors of the Caucasian (Homo sapiens). The word rkh (name for Albino race) and forerunner of the word race, is pre-fixed with the letter "n", which brings the word to mean "no to Albinos (Caucasians)". When some words are pre-fixed with "a", "e" or "i" vowels, the same tends to be regarded as without, as can be seen in the words a-sexual or i-religious (irreligious). This word is of

Egyptian origin, disseminated throughout the world via the Egyptian teachings called masonry.

Can you now see the reason the Caucasian race had to be placed in the cave? One of the many deceits brought on by the cavemen, is linguistic distortion. The Trojan horse is only a drop in the bucket in the arsenal of deception and lies brought to the planet by the Caucasian race. The Trojan horse story is a metaphor like all other in the Greek literary arena.

The character called Superman is alternate version of Jesus, Samson or the Hercules character. Superman's alter ego is called Clark Kent, Batman's alter-ego is Robin, while Jesus' alter ego is a character known as Dark-La (Dracula). The word dark provides us with the first portion of the name Dark-la (Dracula), meaning, prince of darkness. Dracula is the opposite of Jesus; remember Jesus is the alpha (good) and the omega (evil).

The above concept is known as N-khb (Incubus) and S-khb (Succubus). The letter "n" is for no or negative and the letter "s" for yes or affirmative. The same blood Jesus offers to prolong life is the same blood sought by Dracula to prolong life.

Jesus is the prince of light, **John 8:12**

Jesus' alter-ego is the prince of darkness, **Isaiah 14: 16**.

Jesus: Offers blood for eternal life (light)
Dracula: Seeks blood for eternal life (darkness)

We cannot mention the story of Dark-la (Dracula) without mentioning the story of Franken Stein. Like Dracula, Franken Stein is a riddle explaining the identity of the companions of the cave, who are also called Hebrews. The story says that a demented doctor name Franken Stein robbed the cemetery (cave) of cadavers, which later used to make a monster (chaotic society).

The monster needed a brain; the doctor therefore enlisted the brain of a murderous thief into the head of the monster. The brain of the thief is the brain of Prometheus (Jesus, Caucasian), the one who came as a thief, **Rev 16: 15.**

The monster is nothing but an alternate depiction of a society in chaos, the Christian or capitalist society. This story first appeared on the scene on/around 1911, under the Hebrew name Dar Gulam, meaning, House of the children (of Israel).

The children of Israel are the ones referred to by Jesus when he asks to "suffer the children to come to me"; the same children taught the fire (knowledge) by Socrates, the very same children given toys (fire) by Santa Claus. We must remember what Plato (Paul) said in his Timaeus (Timothy?).

"The Egyptians (Afrikans) used to refer to them as children".

It must be borne in mind, that, all Caucasians are children of Israel (cavemen). This only means that they are all Caucasians (cavemen). The name Israel is the English contemporary pronunciation of the Egyptian phrase Asr-il, meaning Prince Asr (Osiris). Similarly, the word Moses (Mesias) is a title of the personage whose name is Asr-Sif (wisdom of Osiris).

Asar-il: Israel Prince Asr (Osiris)
Asar-Sif: Wisdom of Osiris (Moses' name)

Caucasians have managed to corrupt and distort any and everything on which they have laid hands. Moses is only one of the many faces of Jesus the cavemen.

Mesias (Moses) was learned in all the Teru (Tora) of the Egyptians, **Acts 7: 22.**

Mas: Mesias (Moses), Mesiah
Teru: Tora (Egyptian wisdom)

The story of Jesus (cavemen) is a riddle, of which the cavemen and their empire are the central theme. There has never been a man named Jesus, Moses, Solomon or Muhammad who ever walk this earth. These characters are all separate and distinct characteristics of the evolutionary process of the Caucasian and his Arab brethren. We learn how treacherous these two brethren are by nature, no amount of religion can change that. Can you make a lion into a vegetarian? The cavemen are the bringers of disaster, hence the story of Pandora's jar.

As the horse was used to enter Troy, the city's fate is thereafter sealed. The horse is a symbol of death and destruction. Have you wondered about the origin of the word hearse? And why the horse is used to pull the dead? This word is a variant of the word horse, that which is associated with death.

Another word, to which one should pay particular attention, is the word w-hite. This word is calligraphic corruption of the Egyptian word and the Biblical name Hit (Heth), father of the Hittite clone (clan), and patron of the Hethonists (Hedonists). These are all of Caucasian genetic denomination, originators of Hethenism pronounced heathenism (religious) and hedonism (political).

Hit: Het, Hittite race
Hit (Heth): Heathen (Hedonism)

The story, around which Jack revolves, is the story of the Caucasian (cavemen) and the building of the Roman Empire. The House (Empire) that Jack built is one such story. The name Jack is one of the many names of god Bacchus. The name Jack evolved from the word Iacchus. Remember like Jesus, Bacchus is an alpha and an omega. Iacchus is the alpha and Bacchus is the omega. The word back, applied to the human body, learns its name from Bacchus.

Iacchus: Jack (alpha)
Bacchus: Back (omega)

The Counsel of Nicaea, or religious organizers as they are better known, must pay attention to human nature and quit the fanaticism that has spilled into politics and sports.

> Once upon a time, there were five men asked to describe an elephant in a dark room. The master or teacher let the first man into the room; he went grab the leg of the elephant and said this is a **tree.**
>
> The second man was allowed into the room. He went to the tail grabbed it and said, to the first man, you are **wrong**, for this is a **rope**.
>
> The third man was allowed into the room and went to the snout of the elephant, grabbed the same and said to the previous two men, ye are both **wrong**, for this is a large **serpent**.
>
> The fourth man was allowed entry to the room. He went straight to the rib cage of the elephant. He grabbed the same and said to the previous three men, the three of ye are **wrong**, this is a **wall.**
>
> Then entered the fifth man into the room and he went to the back of the elephant and climbed saying, to the previous four, ye are all **wrong** for this is a **mountain**.
>
> Upon seeing this, the master teacher turns on the light and said to his prospective students, ye were **right**, while simultaneously ye were **wrong**. The five neophytes laughed at the master and said to him, how can anyone

be right and wrong at the same time? You must be beside yourself, out of your mind.

The master said to them, ye were right as ye described your perception (culture) as it relates to the world. Ye were wrong when ye found each other (cultures) to be wrong. The afore-mentioned analogy is exactly what is wrong with religious, political and sports fanatics. They all claim their religion, culture or team to be not only the best, but also to be the only or absolute truth. This way of thinking is known as dogma, a one dimensional, unilateral and partial thinking.

The child's many faces

The many phases or characteristics of the child (Chaldean) can be numbered by the amount of animals (life-forms) in Noah's ark. This explains the various Biblical characters and the reason for the word pastor (star: steer). The word pastor is derived from the Egyptian word Bas-t, meaning albinism, hence the words bastard and pest.

Bas-t (Albinism): Bast-ard, pest, past-or

The word bastard is not necessarily a person born out of wedlock; it refers to the albinos who were grafted illegitimately, a process called endogamy or incest. Their genetic diseases earned them the title pestilent, fathers of the cavemen or Caucasian race. The return of Pinocchio to see the Blue fiery (fairy) is indicative (symbolic) of the cavemen returning to his origin to seek healing. This return is also known as seeking of the Holy Grail, the Golden flesh (fleece) and Hunt for the missing link. Each child represents a different face in the cavemen's quest for world racial superiority.

Holy Grail
Birth-right
Wizard of Oz
Blue fiery (fairy)
Golden Flesh (Fleece)
Manu-feast (manifest) Destiny

The name of the child continued to change as we see that one day his name is Abram, then Abraham. Another day it is Esau, and then it changes to Edom Adam). Then it is Jacob and later changed to Asr-il (Israel). These changes are not limited at all. In Greek literature Jesus is Adonis one day, then Dionysus another, then Bacchus on the other. He is Socrates one day, then Prometheus the other. All of the afore-mentioned have children (of Israel) or Manu (men) as its central theme. These narratives have been given to us over the years as stories for children, children is how the Egyptians referred the people of the cave.

The above are some of the many names by which Caucasian racial superiority is known. Most people pay little attention to the literary meaning, but the Caucasian's defective psyche does not pay attention and exaggerates or change the meaning. The struggle or race to this goal is often seen in competitions where the winning prize is referred to as World cup (Holy Grail), the symbol of the Holy Grail or the gold medal, the symbol of the Golden Flesh (Fleece).

Flesh: Phonetic variant of the word **Fleece**

The child is known by as many different names, as we have competitions. Socrates, who like Jesus and Prometheus gave the fire to the children (Manu), is one such name or faces of the child. Another biblical character worth mentioning is that of Plato, a faithful follower of Socrates. Plato is the Greek version of the Roman (biblical) Paul (Phallus), a faithful follower of Jesus.

Plato: Biblical **Paul** and faithful follower of Socrates (Jesus).

Plato was the one who reminds us that, the Egyptian

ancestors referred to the cavemen as children (of Israel), as he explicitly reminds us in his Timaeus (Timo-thy).

> When I was a child, I spoke as a child; I understood as a child, I thought as a child, **Corinthians 13: 1.**

> Suffer the children (cavemen) to come to me, then Jesus called a little child (cavemen), the little children (cavemen) were brought to him, **Matt 19: 14.**

> Who then is the greatest (people) in the domain (kingdom) of heaven (elite)? **Matt 18: 1.**

> I will open my mouth in riddles; I will reveal (Masonic secret) things kept secret from the foundation of Roman Empire (world), **Matt 12: 34**.

> I thank you Lord (Prometheus, Jesus) for taking (stealing) this (wisdom) from the wise and the prudent (intellectual) and giving it to the babes (cavemen), **Matt 11: 25**.

> I will destroy the wisdom of the wise (truth), and bring to nothing the knowledge of the prudent (intellectual), **Corinthians 1: 9.**

> Tell your vision to no one; see to it that no one knows it, **Matt 17: 9.**

> Make sure no one identifies you, for if they do they might cave (stone) you back to your life-form, **Quran 18:19.**

The above Christmas tree is also a symbol of the pyramid, better known as the mountain of the Lord. It is indigenous of an arctic environment, shaped as a pyramid for specific reasons; the light at the top represents the all Seeing Eye. Ascension to the top of this mountain represents the pinnacle of knowledge and wisdom, shared among the elite only. There is lots of secrecy revolving around this knowledge, the true history and nature of the cavemen.

The aforementioned information provides us with a clear vision of the relationship of father and son, the Dad (Daud, David) and the Dude (Jesus, Solomon), the Prince. The words Dude and Dad relate to the king and his son the Prince. From this concept the Latin language evolved the title Father-Lis (federal), meaning Father of the Prince. Thus we have the phrase, our father who art in heaven (elitism), the father who granted his wealth to the prodigal son.

Dad (David): King, father
Dude (Jesus): Prince, Son of David

The frost (first) one came out red all over, like a hairy garment, **Genesis 25: 25.**

The above is a deified version of the same caveman seen earlier in this book, the abominable snowman, St Nicholas patron saint of the Nicolaitians (heathens).

This you have which you hate, the deeds of the Nicolaitians, thus you have also those who hold the doctrine (culture) of the Nicolaitians, **Revelation 2: 6, 15.**

Be not like the Nicholatians (heathen), for their culture is vanity. For they cut a tree from the wild (forest), decorate it with silver and gold and affix it with hammer and nail they it may move not, **Jeremiah 10: 2.**

The cavemen are the children to whom Jesus (Socrates, Prometheus) gave fire (wisdom), after stealing the same. The story of such is given to us in riddles seen in the hymnal (Bible). This disclosure of information (knowledge) is called book of "**Revelation**", and is the central theme in the story of Sat-Nikh-La (Santa Claus) on Christ-Mas night, **Revelation 16: 15.** He (Jesus, Santa Claus) come as a thief.

The above biblical quotes are a narrative of the illegal initiation of the cavemen into what is known as masonry. This wisdom or knowledge is known as the Christ-mas gift to the children, a dramatic ritual practiced one a year. Then the thief promises later in the narrative that he will destroy the world many culture's, many wise men and their wisdom. In the hymnal this can be seen when Jesus turns water into wine, something good into something bad.

The initiation is symbolized by the appearance of Santa Claus (Jesus) bringing the stolen knowledge. After revealing the secrets to Manu (children of the cave), Socrates (or Jesus) was put to death. The initiation has a variety of symbolic names, initiation, baptism, circumcision, aqiqa, etc. The Arab culture refers to it as aqiqa, the introduction of the child into the teachings. Aqiqa, baptism, circumcision: Masonic initiation rituals.

Though the religious communities refuse to accept this fact, the truth is, Islam, Christianity, Judaism and all world religions are the result of Masonic teachings. The Biblical and Quranic characters are fictitious, they never existed, if you can find a gravesite for any of these characters, then they may be able to submit an argument.

Masonry: Islam, Judaism, Christianity

There is a specific reason why the hymnal (Bible) would refer to the same character by many different names. The many faces of the child can be seen in all of the fairy-tale stories in which the child is the central figure, and his adventure is the central theme. Stories such as Pinocchio, Jack and Jill, Jack and the Beanstalk, Peter Pan, Huckleberry Finn, Peter Pan, Hansel and Gretel, etc, are all extrapolations of the saga of the cavemen.

Each of the aforementioned stories has been individualized and presented as unique, and from the same, a different religion (oligarchy) and/or political (monarchy) ideology has been presented. Have you wondered why the saying, never argue religion or politics? This is because politics and religion are one and the same; therefore religion (Bible, Church) cannot be separated from re-biblic (republic, state).

Religion: Babel (Church, Bible)
State: Re-biblic (republic, Babelon, state)

Every religion adopted its own form of initiation, everyone has its monarch, and the king is usually the result of endogamy (incest), hence racism. Muhammad is the monarch in Islam, Jesus is the monarch in Christianity, Solomon is the monarch in masonry, Krishna is the monarch of Krishna culture, Buddha is the monarch of Buddhism, Moses is the monarch in Judaism and Zoroaster is the monarch in Zoroastrianism, and the list goes on and on.

Endogamy (incest) has been greatly glamorized by religious fanatics and their Caucasian leaders. The depraved practice called monarchy is the result and intended goal. The compound word monarchy is of Egyptian origin and the same means one race. The Greek word mono is stems from the Egyptian Mun, meaning people of the cave.

Mono: One
Rakh: Arch (Race)

Strangely, the word arch (ark) is the same word from which we derive the words race and Erectus. After producing the albinos, these were sent off to the caves and deserts of west Asia. The sandy desert was occupied by the Arabs and the snowy desert was occupied by the Caucasians, following their evolution from the albino (Homo erectus).

Sandy desert: Occupied by Arab (Ishmael)

Snowy desert: Occupied by Caucasian (Isaac)

We learn the story of these two groups, from literary stories like that of Abraham and his wives Sara and Hagar, who bore two sons, Ishmael (Arabs) and Isaac (Caucasians). The one representing the extreme hot (Arabian sandy desert), the other representing the extreme cold (European snowy desert)

Ishmael (Arabs): Simian (Semitic)
Isaac: (Caucasians): Swine (Hamitic)

These two sons are the subject in the riddle of the prodigal son, known also as Romulus (Cain) and Remus (Abel). The story of the father and two sons is as old as is the Caucasian (cavemen) race. Remember, Adam had two sons Noah had two sons, Moses had two sons, Aries had two sons, and the list goes on and on.

A certain man had two sons (Cain and Abel, Romulus, and Remus) he said: **Luke 15:11.**

He said:

Ask of me anything and I will give you the nations (capitalism) for your inheritance, and the extremes four corners (north, west, south and east) of the earth for your possession, **Psalms 2:8**.

The younger (Cain, Romulus) of them said to his father, give me the portion of goods that falls to me. So he divided for them their livelihood. **Luke 15: 12**.

The father then said:

I will give him a portion among the great (elite), and he (child) will divide the spoils (loot) with the strong (world powers), **Isaiah 53:12**.

> I will cast out nations before you, and enlarge your borders, **Exodus 34: 24**.

> Not many days later the younger gathered all and journeyed to a foreign country and wasted his possessions with lavish living, **Luke 15:12**.

The loot could not be divided between the two because like the Hun (hyena), the younger killed the older; so did Romulus to Remus, Cain to Abel, Claudius to Hamlet, and the list goes on and on. The founding of an empire on the part of the prodigal son (cavemen) comes with a price. At the expense of the other ethnic groups the world over, Caucasians have created a play-ground for themselves.

The Caucasian and the Arab races descend from the African albino, known today as Homo erect-us. These albinos were expelled from Egypt earlier. The story of Moses is one of the most interesting (glamorous), of all the stories that narrate the said expulsion.

The people of the cave are called Hebrews, the word that provides us with the word Hebrew-d (hybrid) and Hebrew-nation (hibernation). Remember, the albino is a hybrid, and their stay in the cave is called hibernation. Is there any reason why non-Caucasians must continue mating with Caucasians?

> Hebrew-d: Hybrid (hybernate)
> Hibernation: Period in the Cave

The boar or swine became their coat of arms or insignia. The symbol means abundance and/or harvest, explaining the origin of the pignata and the piggy bank. This is the reason the consumption of the flesh of the swine became forbidden, because the same is a national symbol.

Big (Pig): Huge (Hog), opulence
Pignata: Icon of opulence
Piggy bank: Symbols of opulence

The swine is the best of all the symbols or totems used to represent the people of the cave. The word swine is evolved from the Egyptian word sin, a word that has many variants and meanings, swine being the German pronunciation. The word swoon is the plural form of the word swine. The Sinai Mountain, the sin-Gog (synagogue) and the sinit (senate) are only a few examples of the swine totem.

Sin: Swine, swoon
Sinai: Related to the swine
Sinit: Senate (fraternity, brotherhood)

We must bear in mind that Jesus' senate (administration) is represented by his twelve (12) disciples, sitting with him at his roundtable called Last supper. This is the reason the Latin word sinit (senado) has come to mean "supper, dinner". The Spanish language however has over the years, changed the spelling to "cenado", also meaning "supper, dinner". Today we don't say the president's senate; we say the president's administration.

The swine, as said earlier, is the Caucasian symbol of fertility, harvest and abundance. Early Greeks wore helmets shaped as the board's head whenever they went to war. So, this totem is not exclusive to one segment of the Caucasian race. The boar's head was the helmet of choice, since the boar is a fierce fighter, **Exodus 15: 3**. The Boars (Boers) of South Africa are a living monument to this fact.

Boars/Boers: Caucasians of South Africa

This boar is also a totem of Aries, the god of war and his followers the Aries-t-khart (aristocrat) and the Arians (Aryans). All Caucasians are Arians (Aryans), just as all Caucasians are Czeu-s (Hebrews). Judaism and Aryanism relate more to their nature and race, than to their religious ideology.

Arie-s: God of war
Arie-s-t-khar-t: Aristocrat
Arie-n: Aryan (warmonger)

The dog (Lycaon: Legion) and the hog (Hebrew) are two of the most widely used totems in the Caucasian (cavemen) saga. When read carefully, the Quran and the Bible mention these two symbols in the form of codes, as if revealing some hidden secrets concerning the people of the cave.

Hog: Swine
Dog: Lycian (Legion)
Gog: Cauc (Caucasian)
Magog: Magic (Caucasian culture)

The dog has two names; the one is canine (people descendants of Cain) or Canaanite, while the other is Lycian (Legion) or Lycaon. The Lycaon is the name of the Afrikan wild dog, this word gave us the word Legion.

Lycaon (Lycian: Legion): African wild dog

Another face of the child that usually goes unexplored and unchallenged is the character we have all come to know as Solomon. This face is so widely known, because Caucasian culture has modeled itself from their understanding of the Egyptian wisdom. Remember, all the characters represent the same cavemen. We should now analyze the following and maybe we'll see further than our hands can reach.

The meek shall inherit the earth,
Jesus Mathew 5:5
Solomon Psalms 37: 11

You are my son; today I've begotten you,
Jesus Acts 13: 33
Solomon Acts 2: 7

Out of Egypt I've ordered my son,
Jesus Mathew 2: 15
Solomon Hosea 1: 11

I open my mouth in riddles (parables),
Jesus Matthew 13: 35
Solomon 78: 2

My God, why have you forsaken me?
Jesus Matthew 27: 46
Solomon Psalms 22: 1

In your hands I commend my spirit,
Jesus Luke 23: 46
Solomon Psalms 31: 5

If anyone enters by me will go in and out and find green pasture,
Jesus, John 10: 9

He makes me to lie down in green pasture,
Solomon, Psalms 23: 2

Jesus son of David,
Matthew 15: 22

The above analysis is only a partial account of the things alleged to have been said by Jesus, as well as by Solomon. Why is, Jesus called son of David in the hymnal (Bible)? This separation of characters by name is also seen in the separation of the Jewish culture from the Christian culture. Jesus is a Jew (Hebrew), why is he and his followers called Christians? Jesus says to have come only for the house of Israel, the so-called Czeu (Jew).

The apparent similarity between Jesus and Solomon is explained as Jesus says that if you have heard of Moses, then they had heard of Me, since the two characters are one. The fact of the matter is religion is the opiate of Manu (man), as stated by that Caucasian communist name Karl Marx. Bear in mind also that, capitalism and communism are the two sides of the same damned coin.

There was once a scorpion sitting at the edge of a pond, lying in wait. There came a frog, the scorpion says to the frog, could you take to the other side of the pond? The frog was very reluctant and said to the scorpion, no, for if I do you shall sting me and I will drown. The eloquent scorpion says to him, why should I sting you? For if I do, you will drown and so would I.

This made sense to the frog who gladly invited the scorpion to hop on his back. Half-way through the journey, the scorpion stings the frog who as he sinks to his death says to the frog: This makes no sense, there is no logic to this action since you will drown behind me. The charming scorpion responds saying, this has nothing to do with reason or logic, my dear friend, and it is in my nature to be deceitful and wicked.

The above story is a clear description of the relationship held between the Caucasian and the rest of the human race. It is in the nature of the Caucasian to be deceitful and wicked. This appears to be an alternate version of the story of the lady who rescued the snake from the cold of a wintery snowy day.

The Circus (Church), or Noah's ark

The story of Noah's ark is one of the oldest and most fascinating. The one question that always arises is, did Noah really build an aircraft carrier type ship in seven (7) days?

> Seven days from now I will rain on the earth for forty days and forty nights, **Genesis 7:4**.

> After seven (7) days the flood-waters came on the earth, **Genesis 7:10**.

If the above holds true, then Noah must have been the busiest man in the history of the planet. Noah is then instructed to get two animals of every species. The next question, how did Noah get and fit two whales in this alleged ark? The answer to this question is in the mind of the questioned, this story is only a riddle (parable) as is the entire Bible. There was never a man name Noah, like the other Biblical characters he is fictitious.

Noah's ark and the concept of the word Pastor are related intimately to the animal icons mentioned throughout the hymnal. Stories such as Batman and his bird companion the Robin are a spin-off of hymnal or Bible. Noah and the ark are representatives of the pastor (leading animal) and his flock or church.

The word Church as is visibly clear is derived from the word Cir-ce (Xir-xi), the name of a queen of the island who converted the eleven disciples of Odysseus (Jesus?) into swoon (pigs). They were later referred to as Lycian (Legion) thereafter.

The name Cir-ce (Xir-xi) also provides us with the words circus, circle and circum (discus, round), hence the circus-m-ci-sion (roundtable discussion, picnic). This word has come to play a very important role in literature; it is also the name of a king mentioned in the book of **Esther 10: 1.**

Xir-xi (Cir-ce): Cir-cus, Chur-ch, circum

Cir-ce is an alternate version of the Old Dame Dob, Eve; she taught the good things (water) and the bad things (vinegar) to the cavemen. While the apple of the original sin only symbolizes knowledge, the vinegar (wine) and water symbolized good and evil or life and death. It is the very same water Jesus turned into vine-gar (vine, wine).

Circus (Circe) is the true name for Noah's ark, which makes it clear to see the relationship of animals and the word circus. This relationship can be seen in the symbolic role played by animals in religious teaching.

> The eleven disciples went away into Galilee to the mountain where Odysseus (Jesus) had appointed for them, **Matt 8: 31.**
>
> The demo-n (people) begged him, allow us to go into (become) the swoon, **Matt 28: 16.**
>
> He made them into apes (Simians, chimps) and swoon (Ham, champs), **Quran 5: 60.**
>
> Chimp: Ape, simian
> Champ: Wild boar, swine
> Champion: Children of the wild

The hairy men were them called Berbers they received sanitation and hygiene among Egyptians. The centers for sanitation and hygiene are called clean-ic (clinic) and the Berber's shave (Barber shop).

Berber shave: Barber shop.

The word zoo which refers to animal grouping, is related to god Zeus, the leader of the Olympians, hence the zeu-diac (zoo-diac). This is by no means a coincidence. The life-form of the cavemen is similar to that of the animals of the filth (field). The word field is a phonetic variant of the word filth (fouled), the smell of the cavemen, according to their father.

Filth: Field (fouled)

The smell of my son is the smell of the animal of the filth (field), **Gen 27: 27.**

The swine is also known as champ, which actually means pig, boar, swine, etc. This word is of Egyptian origin. The history of this word must be first established, it is derived from the Egyptian word kham (ham), meaning swine, pig or boar.

Kham (ham): Swine, pig, boar

The word camp (champ) is campus in the Latin language and campo in the Spanish language. This word means field, the word campo-n (champion) is a derivative meaning, children of the field (wild). The bell used to summon the Christian flock is known as camp-n (campana) in the Spanish and Latin languages. It is the same bell worn by the steer (pastor), leading animal of the filth (field) to graze, the same bell used in the savage ritual known as boxing. The afore-mentioned is only an example of the Caucasian expertise in the glamorizing of things.

The animal of the filth (field) is the central theme in the

story of Noah's ark, known to children as Old McDonald's Farm. Each of the animals represents a different characteristic of the people of the cave. The George Orwell's novel Animal farm is a drama of the detailing the cavemen's rebellion against their kin, known as the Pastor (King David). The story is said to be a dramatization of the Bolshevik take-over of what was later known as U.S.S.R.

Though George Orwell (Eric Blair) attempts as disguising the story as communism, his novel a mirror image of what happened when George Washington and the rest of those animals rebelled against their British parents. The said Pastor (king) is dethroned, hence the feudal period known as family feud. It was relived during the war between England and the United States of America, for the separation of the latter from the former.

The children of Noah play a very central role, even though they are an alternate version of the children of Abraham, the two sons of Adam, etc. The value here is in their names. These two, whose names are Sam (Shem) and Kham (Ham), gave us the words sam-ian (Simeon, simian) and ham (swine). These two represent the ape (chimp) and swine (champ) into which the cavemen and the Arab were converted, by queen Xirxi (Circe). Strangely, Xir-xi is said to be a King (masculine) in the book of Esther. The Quran reminds us,

> King Xir-xi imposed tribute (tax, thithe) throughout the empire (kingdom), **Esther 10: 1**.

> Not those embittered (swine) and those deceived (ape), **Quran 1: 8, 9.**

> Ham: Swine (Hebrew)
> Sam: Simian (ape) (Arab)

The name Sam is the origin of the names Shem, Simian

(Simeon) and I-Sam-il (Ishmael, son of Abraham). The Word simian (Simeon) is by no means a co-incidence, remember they were made into apes and swoon, Sam (Shem): Simian (Simeon), I-Sam-il (Ishmael), Samuel.

Have you ever wondered why every Christian riddle, anecdote, analogy or parable, uses a field animal as icon? This is simply because of the cavemen; they are of field-animal like characteristics. This is also why the Muslim Quran does exactly the same; the animals represent the many beast-like characteristics of Sam (Simian) and Ham (Swine).

The Pastor (leading field animal) of the Circus (church), is emblematic of the steer or leading field animal. The Pastor represents the star (steer) of Jesus, again, the leading animal of the field.

> If anyone enters by me, will go out and find green pasture (field, wilderness), **John 10: 9.**

> He makes me to lie down in green pastures (field, wilderness), **Psalms 23: 2.**

The green pasture mentioned above, is the same pasture seen in the drama (ritual) we call golf. This ritualistic drama is equally symbolic of the king clubbing his son into the cave; this cave is represented by the hole (holy?), **Job 30: 6.** The words golf and the club (rod), originated in the Egyptian compound Khu-alif, later known as khalifa in the Arabic language. The golf club represents the rod mentioned in the book of Psalms.

> Khu-alpha (khalifa): Golf, clof (club)

> Your rod (club, omega) and your staff (guidance, alpha), they con-fort (balance) me, **Psalms 23**

The steer (star) carries a bell around the neck, the church or circus bell. This indicates that the other animals must summoned around him, or follow him. This bell is the one used to summon the multitude or mass.

> Star (of David): Steer (leading field animal), starry, story

The star is a totem of Jesus, the cavemen. The words steer and starry (story) learn their name from the word star. This word is of Egyptian origin, and the same means son of sat (Seth). The plural form of this word is Stan (Satan), meaning children of Sat (Seth). .

> Sta-r (star): Child of Sat (Seth)
> Sta-n (Satan): Children of Sat (Seth)

The bell carried by the steer (star) or pastor is better known as jungle bell, in reference to the field animals. Its chime is called jingle, hence the phrase, jingle bell. The compound word jungle learns its origin from the words Zion-Cleo, meaning Zion-haven and making reference to the cavemen's habitat.

> Zion-Cleo: Jun-Gle
> Jungle bell: Call to religious gathering

The story of Tarzan the Ape-man (Trojan the Abo-min) is presented wrapped in such beautiful package that it is difficult to resist. This is another extrapolation of the cavemen's saga. Notice how the adulteration and alteration of words change the perception of the afore-mentioned stories.

> Trojan the Abo-min: Tarzan the Ape-man

Deception is the cavemen's only effective tool, through

deception they change perception. Such was the case of Odysseus, known among the gods as the cunning trickster. The perception of the people has been changed, evident in the change of idiom and language. We later learn that the destruction of the language and culture of the people the world over became a reality.

> Let us (cavemen) go down (from the city on a hill) and there confuse their (other cultures) language, **Gen 11:** 7.

> You (cavemen) have perverted the words, **Jeremiah 23: 36.**

Another animal named after the albino (alpine), is the Alpha-nut (elephant). This animal is associated to the prowess of the child in question. The child's army is powerful; the elephant is associated to his victories in war campaigns. This elephant is also symbolic of contemporary war-tank.

> Elephant: War tank (giant)

The military power amassed by the child, consists of soldiers called n-fant (infant), hence the infant-ry. Remember, the Caucasian was referred to as children. The Egyptian phrase n-fant however, means, lacking intellect or wisdom. Do you now see why children are related to lacking wisdom? Jesus (Prometheus) then steals this wisdom and gives the same to the children (infant, manu), hence the original sin.

> N-fant (infant): Infant (dwarf), elf (alpha)

The child born, is also represented by a star called dies-astro (disaster), meaning star of light; and sin-astro (sinister), meaning "star of ignorance (wickedness)".

Dies-astro (disaster): Star god (light)
Sin-astro (sinister): Moon-goddess (darkness)

Finally, he is known also as khat-astro-f (catastrophe), meaning shining star of the father. Can you now see how the Caucasian race has managed to distance Christianity from facts?

Khat-astro-f (catastrophe)

The consequences of the arrival of the star continue. Another title used by the circus (church) on a daily basis, is the title of min-astro (minister). This title is also famous among politicians, now; do you really believe that separation of church from state is possible?

Min-Astro: Minister

The title min-astro (minister) is the same title from whence Caucasian language derives the word mun-astro (monster), a variant of the word Munster.

Mun-Astro: Monastery, monster

As can be seen in the above, the star that shone at the birth of Jesus (cavemen) carries many names (meanings). One such name is the name or meaning monster, pronounced monastery. The leader or administrator of the monastery is the minister or monster.

Min-Astro: Ministry

The greatest trick ever pulled by the devil (debil, double), is to convince the world of his non-existence.

The woman, who saved the child's life, is sometimes known as the old Dame Dob. The Old Dame Dob is the alleged Good Samaritan whose gender sometimes changes, and is sometimes portrayed as good as well as evil. This can be seen when it is said that she anointed Jesus with oil, meaning she taught him wisdom, **Acts 7: 22.** Then she raised Moses and taught him the forbidden wisdom.

> Old Dame Dob: Good Samaritan (**Luke 4:** 7)
>
> Jack (Adam) and Jill (Eve) went up a hill
> To fetch a pail of water (wisdom)
> Jack fell down and broke his crown
> And Jill came tumbling after
> Then up Jack got and off did trot
> That old Dame Dob
> Who patched his nob
> With vinegar (evil) and water (good)
> (**See Revelation 3:11-12**)

> A woman came to him having an alabaster flask of very costly fragrant oil (wisdom); a woman of Samaria came to draw water. Jesus said to her: Give me a drink (wisdom). The woman of Samaria said to him: How is it that you, being a Czeu (Jew) asks a drink of me, a Samaritan woman? **John 4:** 7, **9; Matt 26:** 7.

The book of **Luke 10: 30** speaks of the Good Samaritan as male, while the same book speaks of the Good Samaritan as female, **Luke 4:** 7. The knowledge of good and evil is the same wisdom Prometheus gave to Manu (man). The Good Samaritan's gender is not really an issue, except with religious fanatics and Caucasian male supremacists who understand not the nature of literature.

In the case of Czeus-f (Joseph) the Samaritan was the king or Pharaoh of Egypt, while in the case of Moses it was both male and female. The female who retrieved him from the river, gave him to another female who raised him in the Pharaoh's or king's household. In the case of Silenus the Good Samaritan is King Midas. Like the story of the old Dame Dob, there are many stories intended for the children or people of the cave. The story of Pinocchio is the story of the Phoenician, the word from where we derive the name Pinocchio.

Phoenix-ia: Pinocchio

The story says that the child (cavemen) was made with genetic deficiency in a leper-tory (laboratory). He then wants to return to see his ancestry, in order to correct the genetic mishap. This in essence explains why the fields of medicine and health are the two greatest ever in Caucasian capitalism. When the Caucasian is healed (w-holed), he is then said to be hole (holy) from his blood pathogen. This is known as the Hole (holy) Gra-il (grain, gene, seed)

Heal (hole): Holy (hole)
Gra-il (Grail): Grain, brood, scion

The word Phoenixia gave us the name for many other animals of the field; it gave us the word finch, and the word penguin. Strangely, the penguin like the cavemen belongs to an arctic (cold) environment. The word pink relates to the color of the skin of the Albino or Caucasian people. This shade is attributed to those of the feminine gender, while the blue sought by Pinocchio is attributed to the masculine gender.

Phoenix: Pink
Phoenixia: Pinocchio
Phoenix: Finch (pink)

Phoenixian: Penguin (arctic bird)

Pinocchio (Phoenix-ia) seeks the Blue Fiery (fairy), known as Hades (Roman Pluto), the god of the neter-world (n-ther: underworld). This story like the others is an alternate version of the saga of the cavemen. The story of the phoenix bird tells us that this bird goes back to the desert close to its dying time. As it dies, it becomes a ball of fire, leaving only ashes behind. Births (birds) generally symbolize birth of the origin of the word bird suggest, this is seen in the phrase "the birds and the bees".

The ashes left behind by the dead become another phoenix bird, thus the Roman Empire regenerates. One day the empire is known as the Roman Empire, next it is known as Spanish empire, then as British Empire, the Ottoman Empire, and so on. They all continue the Roman Empire's goal of Caucasian male supremacy, lead by a brotherhood whose real goal is always covert.

The hairy-man who rules the Empire is to be sanitized during initiation into masonry; this is why the warning to the king says that the child's head and body will remain unshaven. This is also the reason Oedipus' tale says he would sire children who would make man shudder, as these look upon his children.

The red (pink skin), hairy cavemen who stole the knowledge and gave the same to children (cavemen), is dramatized annually by a character we have come to know as Santa Claus. The gifts to the children represent this stolen knowledge, while the children (of Israel) are indicative of the cavemen. The cavemen were no longer considered children, soon as they were initiated into the wisdom of the Egyptians. This wisdom is known today as masonry. The phrase, Manu know Theo Self was inscribed on the temple.

Manu: Cavemen

Know: Learn, ponder
Theo (thy): Science of opposites
S-Alpha (self): Albino (Homo erectus)

The education of the cavemen consisted of them learning their origin and their nature. The Theo self consists of the nature of good and evil that is their very essence. The reason for learning the science of opposites is for the Caucasian to learn to balance himself, his evil nature, and not tilt that balance, **Quran 55: 4, 7; Bhagavat Gita 5:20.**

The first step in the initiation is the shaving of the entire body, a tradition learned by monks becoming members of a temple. The rebel, whose head is untouched by a razor, is a sign of defiance to these teachings.

> The first one came out red all over, like a hairy garment, **Genesis 25: 25**.

> He was a hairy man wearing an apron, **II Kings 1: 8**.

> Does not nature itself teach us that if a man has long hair (hairy) it is a dishonor to him? **1 Corinthians 11:14.**

> God will wound the head of his enemies, the hairy scalp of the one who persists in his rebellion, **Psalms 68: 21.**

> We will hold him by his lock (of hair), that lying wicked locks, **Quran 95: 15-16.**

> We shall gather on that day (all) the wicked blue-eyed, **Quran 20: 102**.

The above-mentioned lock is typically seen in the Czeus (Jewish) traditionalist and the Krishna philosophy devotees, as well as among the Rastafarians. The initiate is given twenty-one (21) degrees, each of which has a numeric and a symbolic value. These twenty-one (21) degrees became today's alphabet; of course the cavemen added letters, thus corrupting the teachings.

The 0 + 21 degrees became the foundation for western (cavemen) culture. The age twenty-one (21) became the age of maturity; twenty-one became the number of years for completion of studies, first grade to PhD; twenty-one became the total gun salute rounds upon consummation (death), Black Jack, and so on.

There are another twelve (12) honorary degrees known as, Labors of Hercules implicating altruism. These degrees are symbolic of humanitarian and/or altruistic efforts, and are represented by Jesus' twelve (12) disciples. These twelve degrees are combined with the twenty-one (21) worthy degrees to obtain thirty-three degrees, the alleged age of Jesus and the highest degrees achieved in the teachings of masonry.

> We have given you (cavemen) very little knowledge (33 of 360, 1/10) **Quran 47:12.**

0 + 21: Degrees given to the cavemen
12: Honorary degrees, Labors of Hercules
33: Maximum degrees allowed to cavemen

Once the initiate completes the studies he acquires self-ation (salvation) or knowledge of self, called salvation today. The word self is adopted by the Latin language as selva, meaning jungle, wilderness. This is no coincidence; the jungle or the wild (wilderness) is in the very self (nature) of the cavemen.

Self (selva): Jungle

Self-ation: Salvation

The star (light) which represents the child is called Maji-ast (majesty), meaning light of a maji (magi, imagery). The word magi evolves from the name of goddess May, in whose honor the 5th month of the year is named. She is the goddess of illusion and illustration, hence the words i-mag (image) and magic.

Ast (Seth): Light (Lux-fir: Lucifer)
May (Mag): Illusion/illustration goddess

The name Magog is a visibly clear derivation of the word magic, Magog is the Hebrew version of the Greek god Atlas, son of Iapetus (Japheth). This god is the one who carries the burden of the world upon his shoulders.

Iapetus (Japhet), son of Noah **Gen 10:1**
Magog, son of Iapetus (Japhet) **Gen 10: 2**

He has the whole world, in his hand he has the whole wide world, he has the whole world in his hands. The ever-present companion of Magog is Gog, meaning, blind (blue-eyed) or spiritless (non-intellectual). This name evolved from the Latin word caecu, the Spanish language adopted it as cieco (ciego) meaning, non-vision. The Hebrew language then pronounces it as Gog, hence the word gog-gles, meaning blindfold.

Caecu (Cieco): Caucus (blind)
Caucus (Gog): blind (Blue-eyed)

Gog (Cauc) is also known as Samson, the blind man who died at his own hands. This character is known to Greeks as Hercules, the one who destroyed his entire family when he became blind by rage.

Gog: Hercules
Magog: Atlas

The word caecu-s (cieco) gave us a variant, this variant is pronounced caucus, hence the word Caucasian. A Caucasian is anyone possessing blue eyes. In fact the words blond and blind are direct derivations of the name Baal (Phal: Phallus), yielding the word blue later. These both make reference to the Caucasian, a mark by which Cain (Canaanites) is known.

The lord set a mark upon Cain, **Genesis 4:15**.

Blind: Blue-eyed
Blond: Yellow-haired
Cauc: Gog (Gog-gles), Caucasian

The trick practiced by religious fanatics is, to claim originality and authenticity, neither of which is true. Western and near eastern religions are based on the so-called Greek myth, something stolen from Egypt, **Quran 15:18**. The stolen literature is the central theme in the story of Prometheus, who stole fire (knowledge) and gave the same to Manu (men). It is the reason for the expulsion of the Adamites (Caucasians, Hebrews) from Egypt; it is the reason Jesus (Socrates) is put to death.

The re-emergence of the child is marked by a culture known as the New Testament which marred the planet. This so-called New Testament is the philosophy devised by the cavemen to rule what they call the New World. Combined, the New World and New Testament equals the New World Order.

New World: Cavemen's amazement
New Testament: Cavemen's philosophy

New World Order: Cavemen's imposition

The newly develop culture would be known as the phallic (penis) culture, one whose initiation begins with something called the circu-m cision of the phallus. The phallus is thereafter venereal ized (venerated) through a set of subtle rituals, which will be covered in the segment that follows.

The Phallic culture

The phallic culture is a culture around which everything related to sex and sexual paraphernalia revolve. The phallic culture has its origin in the Egyptian culture. Caucasians with their wicked nature have managed to vilify it. They have taught over the years, a philosophy in which its initiation is the mutilation of the phallus. This all is supposed to be symbolic. The mutilation is called circumcision, an initiation ritual. However, like all else, the cavemen interpreted its meaning on a physiological level.

> Every male among you (cavemen) shall be circumcised (scalping of the phallus), **Genesis 17: 9**.

The story of the murder of Osiris at the hands of is brother Sat (Seth), gave birth to the stories of Cain and Abel, Romulos and Remus, Claudius and Hamlet and many others. The story says that Sat (Seth) murdered and dismembered his brother Asr (Osiris). He then took all the body parts and cast them into the Nile river. The body parts were recovered, all except the phallus (penis), which was swallowed by a salmon fish. This phallus was taken by the fish and evolved into the phallic culture or culture of the testis (Testament).

The phallic culture is characterized by sexual overtone, homosexuality, sexual paraphernalia, incest, pedophilia, pornography and rape, hence the name Testis-ment (Testament) and words venereal and venerate.

Testi-ment (Testament): The phallic culture

The phallic culture uses a doctrine to guide its day to day philosophical views; this doctrine is called the testis-ment (testament), Latin word for groin. The same was so named by the organizers of religion, known as the Counsel of Nicaea, meaning Counsel of the Sinister. It must be clear that there has never been an official registered or documented group by such name, their name is a myth as is the Christian or capitalist culture.

Counsel of Nicaea: Counsel of the sinister

One of the most antique forms of the teachings of the phallic culture is called Khi-Phallus, meaning, consciousness of the phallus. This went on to become the word Ca-Baal, known to most as Cabala. The phrase Khi-Phallus is Egyptian, and is from whence the Latin language learned the word cephalous, meaning brain. Those who became devotees of the teachings were called Dies-Cephalous, pronounced disciples and meaning learned (men) of the phallic consciousness.

Dies-Cephalous: Disciple
Khi-Phallus: Cephalous, Cabala

The so-called testament is an invention of the Caucasian, owing mostly to his lack of psychological (spiritual) comprehension of the Egyptian teachings. The lack of pigmentation is a physiological disease affecting the Caucasian psyche (spirit), sending the same out of balance.

The word venerate is a verbal form of the noun venereal, this word has its origin in the name Venus, the symbolic mother of the Caucasian race. From this name we also derive the words venom and vengeance. Greek lore has it that the Caucasian woman was created by god Czeus (Zeus) as punishment to Prometheus.

Venu-s: Venu-m (venom)

Venus (vengeance) is mine said the Lord, **Romans, 12: 19.**

The beginning of the phallic culture can be seen in the city we have come to know as Bible (Babel) or rebiblic (republic), the city on a hill, **Matthew 5: 14**. The descendants or people of the cavemen are then called Bible-n (Babylon). One can see by the afore-mentioned that the cavemen usually change the phonetics and turn around some symbols (letters) only to disguise truth,

Bible: Hymnal depicting the saga of the cavemen.

Biblen: Babylon (Children or people of the Bible)

The children or people mentioned are known also as children of Israel among other names. We must bear in mind what Plato (Paul) said in his Timaeus (Timothy), "the Egyptians used to refer to us as children".

The city (Empire) on a hill in question is organized under the title re-biblic (republic). Notice the word Babel (Bible) in the compound re-Biblic (republic)? Plato (Paul) later wrote another article called the Re-Biblic, known today as the Re-public.

Plato's Republic: Paul's Re-biblic

The haven is the very top of the hill, also known as the Mountain of the Lord. This mountain is symbolized by the pyramid seen on the United States one (1) dollar bill. The bottom portion of the hill or piedmont is called hell, among other names.

Hill: Upper Mountain
Hell: Lower Mountain
Hall: Dwelling place of the elite (gods)

The dwelling place of the Eli (gods), or as it is called in the French language, elite, is a place called hall. On this hill, symbolically speaking, the wealthiest reside. The lower portion of the mountain is called hell, and the most wretched of the society reside there. These two levels are called Zion-t (Zenith) and Zoar (Jer) in the Bible.

Zion-t (Zenith): Top of the mountain
Zoar-k (Jericho): Foot of the mountain

The cave represents this hell, **Job 30:6**; hence the devil dwells beneath the earth. The Eli (eli-te) dwell today on the seat of Capitalism, known as Capitol Hill, the hill upon which a city is located. Remember that, a city on a hill cannot be hidden, **Mathew 5: 14.**

Capitalism: The phallic culture
Capitol Hill: Seat of Capitalism

The circus (church) played the most important role in the creation of this culture. The Roman world (Empire) erected a building size phallus before their temples. This phallus was called Venerii, and is derived from the name Venus, their goddess of lust (love?). Contemporary culture refers to anything relating to this phallus, as Venereal, hence the word Venerate.

Venerii (Phallus): Venerate, venereal

In order to understand the complexities of the cavemen culture, it is essential that one comprehends the nature of the people of the cave. Their physiology is only a manifestation of their psychology. Afrikans/Egyptians have syche (lower conscience) and Ab-syche (upper conscience), unlike Caucasians who have Conscience and sub-conscience (below conscience).

Sakh: Sage (lower conscience)
Ab-sakh: Psyche (higher conscience)
Sub-sakh: Below (all) conscience

The afore-mentioned words are the Greek version of the Egyptian word Sakh and its variant Sikh, and it means consummation, completion, evolved, etc. The words, sex, seek, ask, sage and the like, have all evolved from this word. The two levels of consciousness are called, conscience and sub-conscience, actually meaning conscience and below conscience. The ab-syche is the superior conscious as is visibly clear in the word ab/up (above).

Ab (Up): Higher, ab-ove
Sub-conscience: Lower conscience

The Afrikans and other ethnic varieties refer to their off-spring as ascendants, because a (family) tree ascends or grows up, not down. Caucasians refer to their off-spring as descendants, meaning to grow down. This explains the way they think as they do and why the Muslim Quran says, we created man in the best essence, then we degraded him to the lowest, from extreme best (melanin), to extreme worst (albino).

Among the greatest problems in religious fanaticism today, is the fact that its adherents claim this exclusive connection to a god and a monopoly on knowledge. All of these religious fanatics claim that their god came to them in the person of their founder. Each group or sect claims that their lore was revealed and written in their native language. What is really disgusting is their claim that God and the angels speak in their native language only.

The only ethnic group in the world that claims the visit of their god without racial over-tone or prejudice is the African. When people built an altar for their culture, they put the image of their ethnicity as the person in which their god visited them. The African is the only ethnic group who build their altar with the ali-ments and ele-ments produced by Mother Nature. And when they claim a visit from their god, it is usually that their god visited them in the spirit of rain, a tree, a plant, food, etc., that is genius.

Ali, Eli: God, highest, etc
Ali-ments: Food (goodness)
Ele-ments: Nature (goodness)

The African principle does not suggest any form of racism, and also evident is the fact that, the others are racists in nature. How can the Counsel of Nicaea (religious organizers) claim that god wants to talk to us through them? That god is racist. Why not visit us then as he visits the others? Are we not worthy enough to merit his/her visit?

These are some of the concepts that must be taught to the African children, and the reason they must be educated by Africans like themselves. Caucasian schools are designed not to educate, but to train (program). This is clearly visible when a student is ask, what is your major? They all respond with something needed in the market, a euphemism for the word plantation.

Market: Euphemism for the word Plantation

The phallic symbol is sometimes represented by the little white cap worn by the Muslims, and called khufi (kuffi), it is supposed to make the person resemble a candle or penis. The name of the capo has its origin in the name Khu-Fu (Cheops), hence the word cap (Cheop); the Catholic religious initiation shaved the very top of the head of the priest during his first few months as a monk, this is called Tonsura. The Hebrew culture, like the Islamic culture, wears a cap called "kippa", a visibly clear variant of the word "kuffi", which also made the person appear as a candle or circumcised penis.

Khu-Fu: Kuf-Fi (kuffi), kippa

The phallus is, again, the symbol of the culture at hand, a pornographic culture. The hymnal (Bible) refers to the knowledge learned in this culture as, the wine of porn-cation (fornication), Testis-ment:

> What is this, a new teaching (New world order)? These men are full of new wine, **Acts 2:13**; **Mark 1:27**.
>
> They gather for grain (teachings) and new wine (New Testament or phallic culture), **Hosea 7:14**.
>
> They will drink and roar (feasts of economic abundance) as with new wine (phallic culture), **Zechariah 9:15**.
>
> The vats will overflow with new wine (sports, play, feasts and celebrations), **Joel 2:24.**
>
> New wine will drip from the mountains and flow from all the hills, **Amos 9:13**.

On that day the mountains (industrialized nations) will drip new wine (phallic culture, Christianity), **Joel 3:18**.

Wail all you drinkers of wine, wail because of the new wine (phallic culture, new testament), **Joel 1:5**.

What has been will be, what has been done will be done, for there is nothing new under the sun, **Ecclesiastes 1:9**.

All nations have drunk the wine (phallic culture) of the wrath of her (Liberty statue) fornication (venerate, venereal), **Rev 18:3**.

They will be entangled among thorns (phallic culture, New Testament), **Nahum 1:10**.

To give themselves to pro-state (prostitution), to the old wine and new (testament), which take away the understanding (is Christianity), **Hosea 4: 11.**

They eat the bread of wickedness and drink the wine of violence, **Proverbs 4:17**.

Therefore, if anyone is in Christianity (Christ), he is in the new world order (New Testament, new creation), **II Corinthians 5:17**.

The grain (economy) is destroyed and the new wine (phallic culture) is dried up. Babylon the great (world power) has fallen, which made all nations drink the maddening wine of her adulteries (phallic culture), **Joel 1:10; Rev 14:8**.

If history is to serve us properly, then the following sonnet on historical lessons is a model. This poem is said to have been written by Percy Bische Shelly. The same appears to be highlighting the results of a previous Afrikan version of a capitalist society.

Ozimandias

I met a traveler from an antique land
Who said: Two vast and trunkless legs of stone
Standing in the desert… Near on the sand,
Half sunk a shattered visage lies, whose frown,
And wrinkled, and sneer of cold command,
Tell us that its sculptor well those passions read
Which yet survive, stamped on those lifeless things,
The hand that mocked them, and the heat that fed them
And on the pedestal these words appear:
My name is Ozimandias, King of kings:
Look at my works, ye mighty and despair!
Nothing beside remains. Round the decay
Of that colossal wreck, boundless and bare
The lone and level sands stretch far away

Percy Bische Shelley

Epilogue

At this point, it is obvious in the mind of the reader that religion of any type is in the business of corrupting. The business of controlling, profiting and with no intellectual value for its prey/victim; it is rather dangerous. This is called prose-lytize, the act of religious conversion, or political conversion of a person to a particular idiosyncrasy.

> You travel the land and sea, seeking to make one proselyte (religious/political convert), but when he is converted he becomes twice the wicked person (child of hell) you are, **Matthew 23: 15.**

The United States of America is going through some changes, changes that are obviously the first part of its fall. Social unrest caused by economic chaos and disagreement will soon lead to rebellion, a typical Caucasian trait. Remember Animal Farm by George Orwell? There is no way of stopping the spinning wheel, or the sun from shining.

Once upon a time there was a lady who owned a restaurant. She had a tremendous problem, she noticed that everytime she hired a chef, she would have complaints from those who patronized her. As she hired a chef she found that she also had to fire him because of the vast amount of complaints.

She had a waitress who was very observant. The waitress said to her, don't you think that it will be better to change your culinary recipe, rather tan changing your chefs? The lady owner took up the suggestion. Following this change, the owner of the said restaurant noticed a tremendous change in the attitude of her patrons. She continued from then on, to focus on improving her recipe, not changing chefs.

What is the point in the above story? People must focus in changing their culture, not changing presidents, governors, senators, mayors and councilmen. If the culture is not changed, the elected official means nothing but a face-lift.

Sources

Holy Bible, King James version
Holy Bible, New International Version
Holy Quran, by Maulana Muhammad Ali
Bhagavat Gita, by Swami Prabhupada
Mithology, by Edith Hamilton
Subterranean Rome, Charles Didier